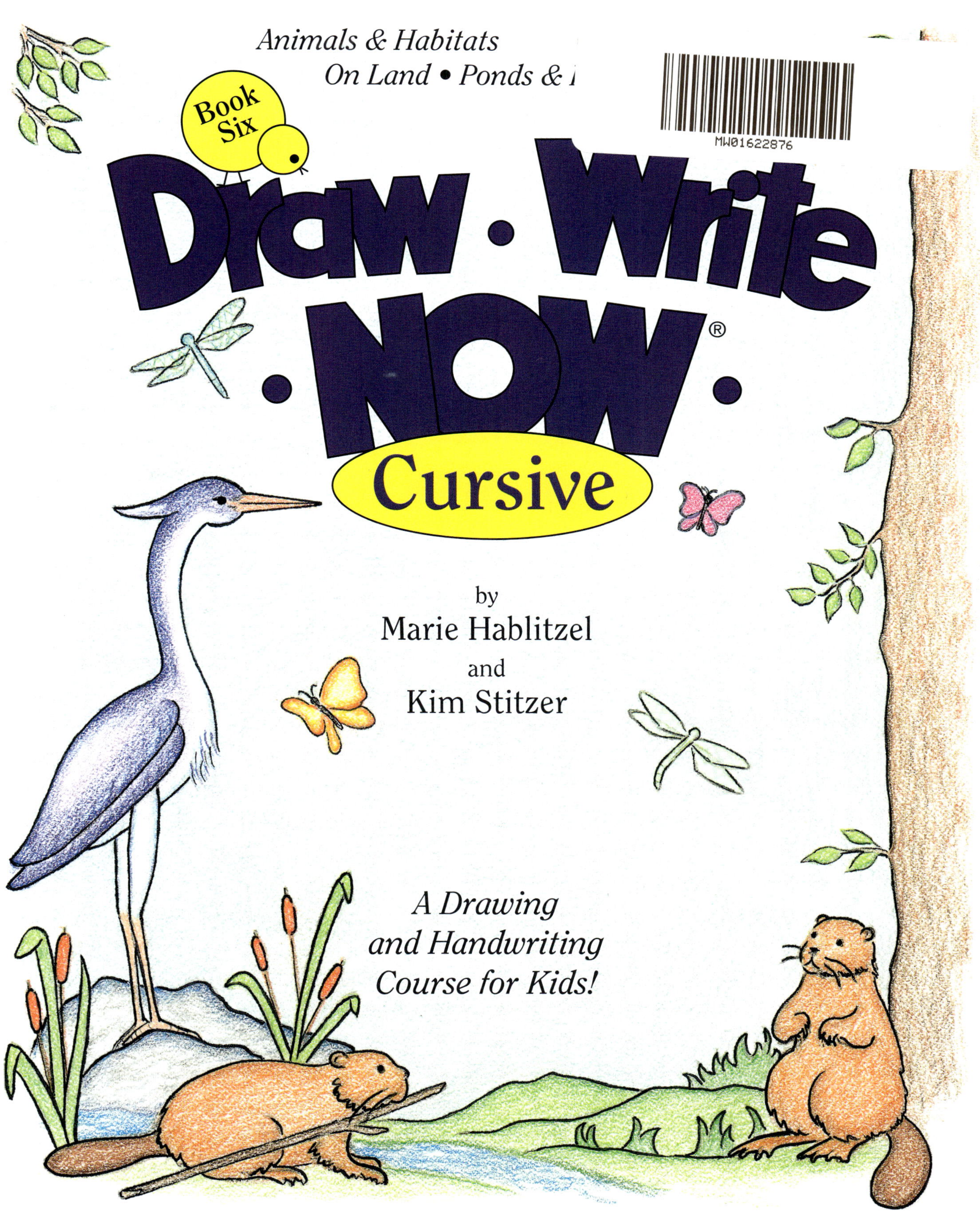

Rainbow Resource Center, Inc. • Toulon, Illinois

Dedicated to...

...my grandchildren.
I have enjoyed drawing with you! — M.H.

...Virginia Crockett — K.S.

Cursive font in this book: Developed by Iris Hatfield, with over 35 years of experience in the handwriting field, New American Cursive improves the process of teaching handwriting through simplified letter forms and allows students to start at a younger age. To learn more about New American Cursive, visit us on the web: www.newamericancursive.com. The drawings are done using Prismacolor pencils outlined with a black PaperMate FLAIR!® felt tip pen.

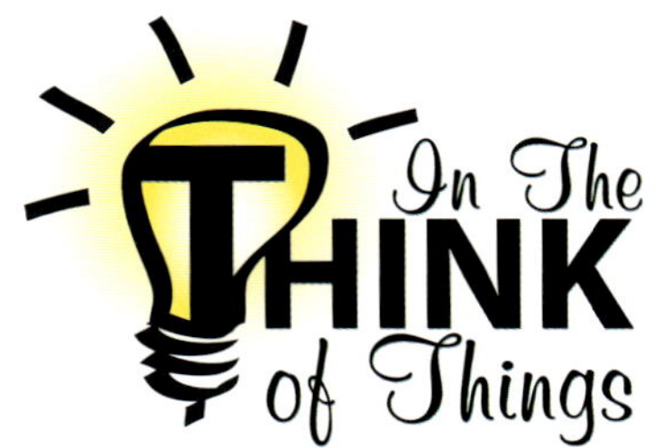

Published by Rainbow Resource Center, Inc.
655 Township Rd 500E • Toulon, IL 61483
Phone: 888.841.3456 • Fax: 800.705.8809
Email: publishing@rainbowresource.com

New American Cursive edition published in 2020.

Book layout by Judy Richardson
Printed in USA

Library of Congress Catalog Card Number: 93-73893

Publisher's Cataloging in Publication Data:
Hablitzel, Marie, 1920 - 2007
Draw•Write•Now®, Book Six: A drawing and handwriting course for kids!
(sixth in series)

Summary: A collection of drawing and handwriting lessons for children. *Book Six* focuses on Animals & Habitats: On Land, Ponds & Rivers, Oceans. Sixth book in the *Draw•Write•Now®* series.

1. Drawing—Technique—Juvenile Literature. 2. Drawing—Study and Teaching (Elementary). 3. Penmanship. 4. Animals — Juvenile Literature. 5. Habitat (Ecology)— Juvenile Literature. 6. Natural History—Juvenile Literature.
I. Stitzer, Kim, 1956 - , coauthor. II. Title.
741.2 [372.6]—dc 19

ISBN: 978-1-942446-15-6

Cursive Edition: First Printing

About this book…

For most children, drawing is their first form of written communication. Long before they master the alphabet and sentence syntax, children express themselves creatively on paper through line and color.

As children mature, their imaginations often race ahead of their drawing skills. By teaching them to see complex objects as combinations of simple shapes and encouraging them to develop their fine-motor skills through regular practice, they can better record the images they see so clearly in their minds.

This book contains a collection of beginning drawing lessons and text for practicing handwriting. These lessons were developed by a teacher who saw her second-grade students becoming increasingly frustrated with their drawing efforts and disenchanted with repetitive handwriting drills.

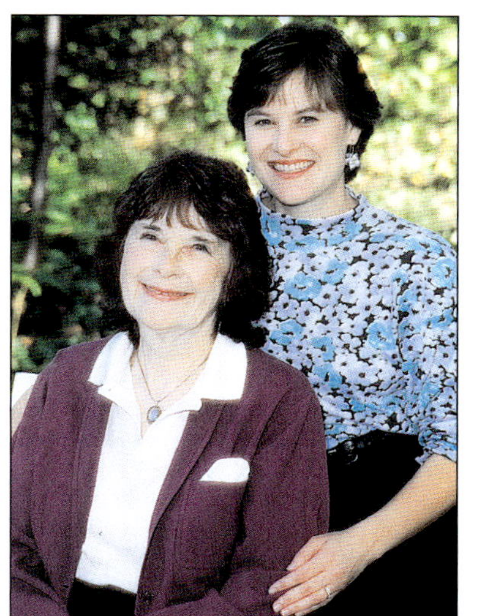

Coauthors Marie Hablitzel (left) and her daughter, Kim Stitzer

For more than 30 years, Marie Hablitzel refined what eventually became a daily drawing and handwriting curriculum. Marie's premise was simple—drawing and handwriting require many of the same skills. And, regular practice in a supportive environment is the key to helping children develop their technical skills, self-confidence and creativity.

As a classroom teacher, Marie intertwined her daily drawing and handwriting lessons with math, science, social studies, geography, reading and creative writing. She wove an educational tapestry that hundreds of children have found challenging, motivating—and fun!

Although Marie is now retired, her drawing and handwriting lessons continue to be used in the classroom. With the assistance of her daughter, Kim Stitzer, Marie shares more than 150 of her lessons in the eight-volume *Draw•Write•Now*® series.

In ***Draw•Write•Now***®, ***Book One***, children explore life on a farm, kids and critters and storybook characters. ***Books Two*** through ***Six*** feature topics as diverse as Christopher Columbus, the weather, Native Americans, the polar regions, young Abraham Lincoln, beaver ponds and life in the sea. In ***Draw•Write•Now***®, ***Books Seven*** and ***Eight***, children circle the globe while learning about animals of the world. ***Books Five*** through ***Eight*** are now offered in a Cursive series!

We hope your children and students greatly enjoy these lessons!

—In the Think of Things

Table of Contents

A table of contents is like a map. It guides you to the places you want to visit in a book. Pick a subject you want to draw, then turn to the page listed beside the picture.

For more information on the ***Draw•Write•Now***® series, see page 3. For suggestions on how to use this book, see page 6.

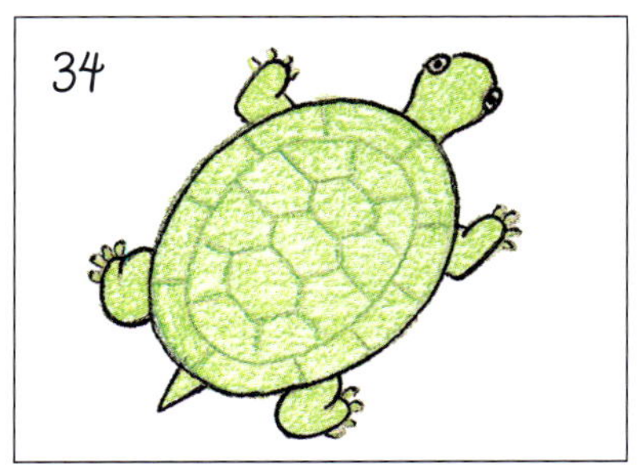
34

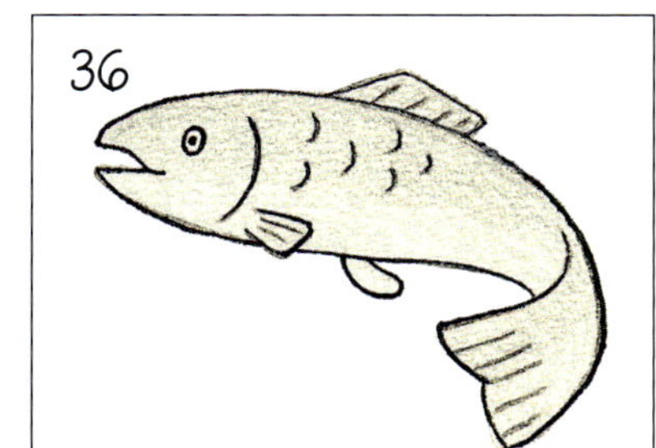
36

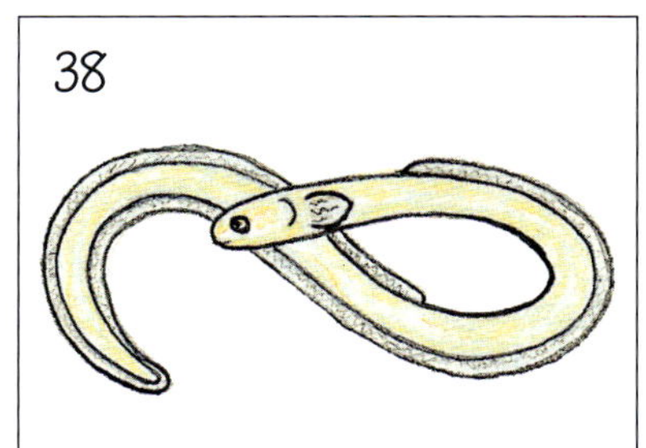
38

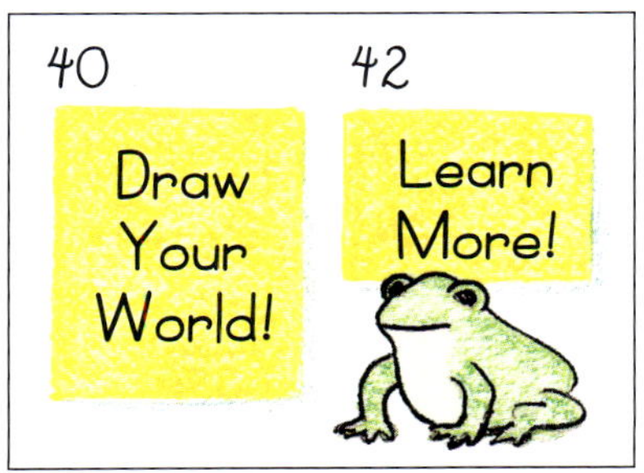
40
42
Draw Your World!
Learn More!

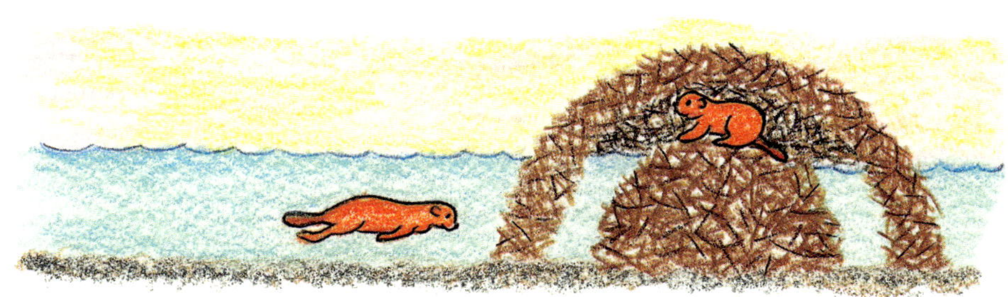

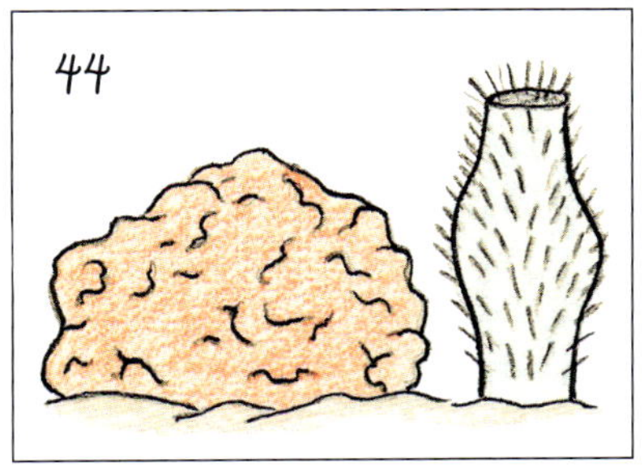
44

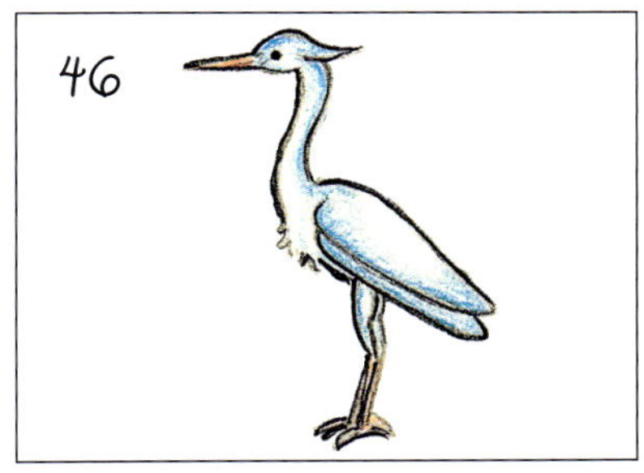
46

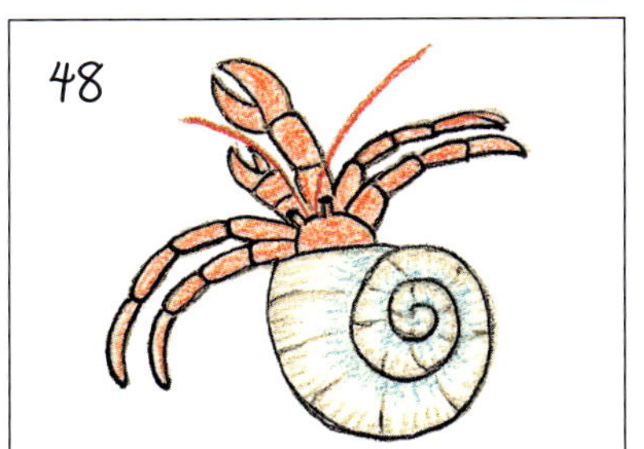
48

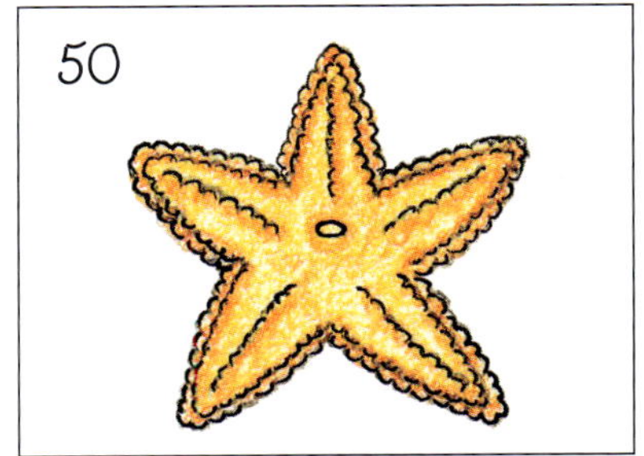
50

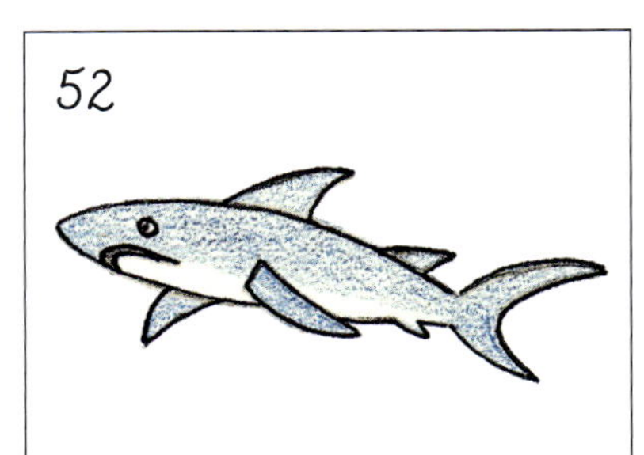
52

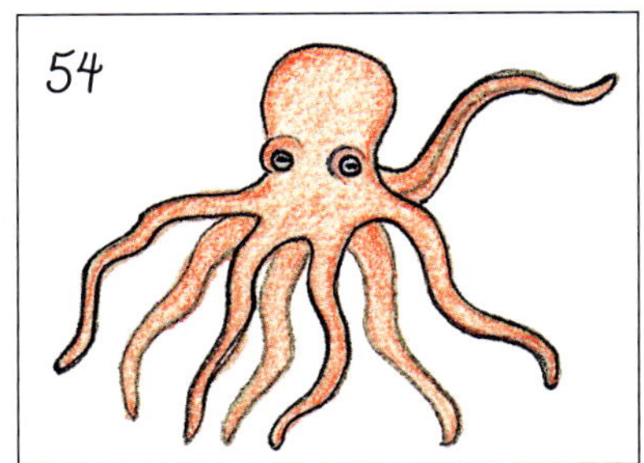
54

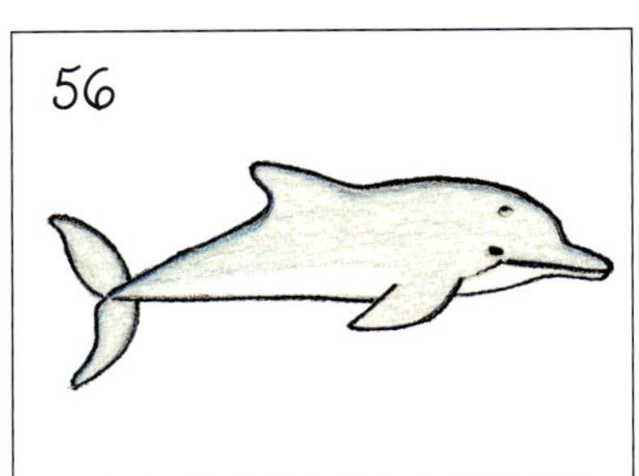
56

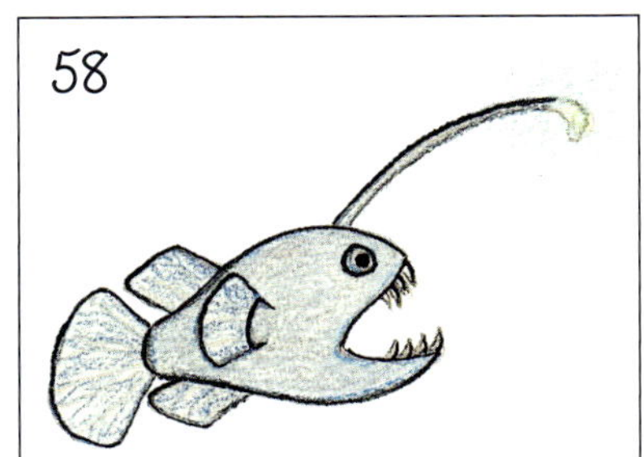
58

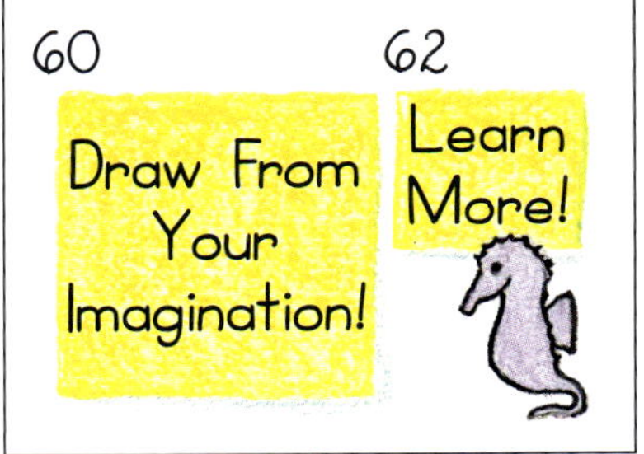
60
62
Draw From Your Imagination!
Learn More!

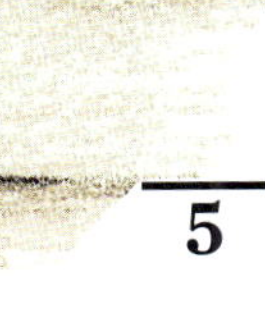

A few tips to get started...

This is a book for children and their parents, teachers and caregivers. Although most young people can complete the lessons in this book quite successfully on their own, a little help and encouragement from a caring adult can go a long way toward building a child's self-confidence, creativity and technical skills.

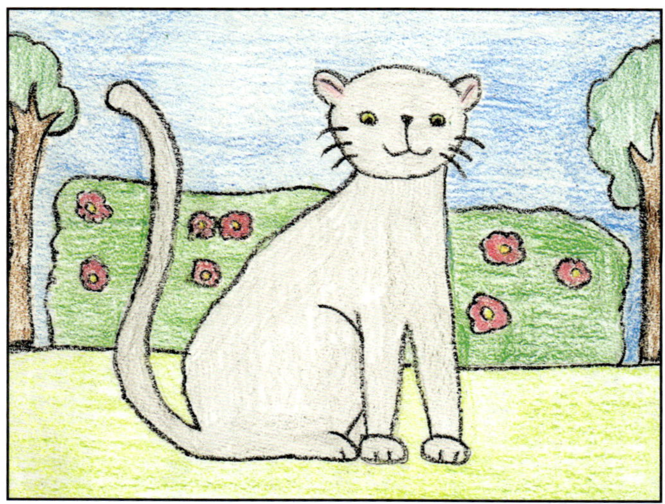

Cat by Lauren Freeny, age 7
from Draw•Write•Now®, Book One

The following outline contains insights from the 30-plus years the authors have worked with the material in this book. Realizing that no two children or classrooms are alike, the authors encourage you to modify these lessons to best suit the needs of your child or classroom. Each ***Draw•Write•Now***® lesson includes five parts:

1. Introduce the subject.
2. Draw the subject.
3. Draw the background.
4. Practice handwriting.
5. Color the drawing.

As presented here, each child will need a pencil, an eraser, drawing paper, penmanship paper and either crayons, color pencils or felt tip markers to complete a lesson.

1. Introduce the Subject

Begin the lesson by generating interest in the subject with a story, discussion, poem, photograph or song. The questions on the illustrated notes scattered throughout this book are examples of how interest can be built along a related theme. Answers to these questions and the titles of several theme-related books are on pages 26, 42 and 62.

2. Draw the Subject

Have the children draw with a pencil. Encourage them to draw lightly because some lines (shown as dashed lines on the drawing lessons) will need to be erased. Show the children the finished drawing in the book. Point out the shapes and lines in the subject as the children work through the lesson. Help the children see that complex objects can be viewed as combinations of lines and simple shapes.

Help the children be successful! Show them how to position the first step on their papers in an appropriate size. Initially, the children may find some shapes difficult to draw. If they do, provide a pattern for them to trace, or draw the first step for them. Once they fine-tune their skills and build their self-confidence, their ability and creativity will take over. For lesson-specific drawing tips and suggestions, refer to *Teaching Tips* on pages 63–64.

3. Draw the Background

Encourage the children to express their creativity and imagination in the backgrounds they add to their pictures. Add to their creative libraries by demonstrating various ways to draw trees, horizons and other details. Point out background details in the drawings in this book, illustrations from other books, photographs and works of art.

Encourage the children to draw their world by looking for basic shapes and lines in the things they see around them. Ask them to draw from their imaginations by using their developing skills. For additional ideas on motivating children to draw creatively, see pages 24–25, 40–41 and 60–61.

4. Practice Handwriting

In place of drills—rows of e's, r's and so on—it is often useful and more motivating to have children write complete sentences when practicing their handwriting. When the focus is on handwriting—rather than spelling or vocabulary enrichment—use simple words that the children can easily read and spell. Begin by writing each word with the children, demonstrating how individual letters are formed and stressing proper spacing. Start slowly. One or two sentences may be challenging enough in the beginning. Once the children are consistently forming their letters correctly, encourage them to work at their own pace.

There are many ways to adapt these lessons for use with your child or classroom. For example, you may want to replace the authors' text with your own words. You may want to let the children compose sentences to describe their drawings or answer the theme-related questions found throughout the book. You may prefer to replace the New American Cursive style used in this book with a different style of cursive or a manuscript style. If you are unfamiliar with the various alphabet styles used for teaching handwriting, consult your local library. A local elementary school may also be able to recommend an appropriate alphabet style and related resource materials.

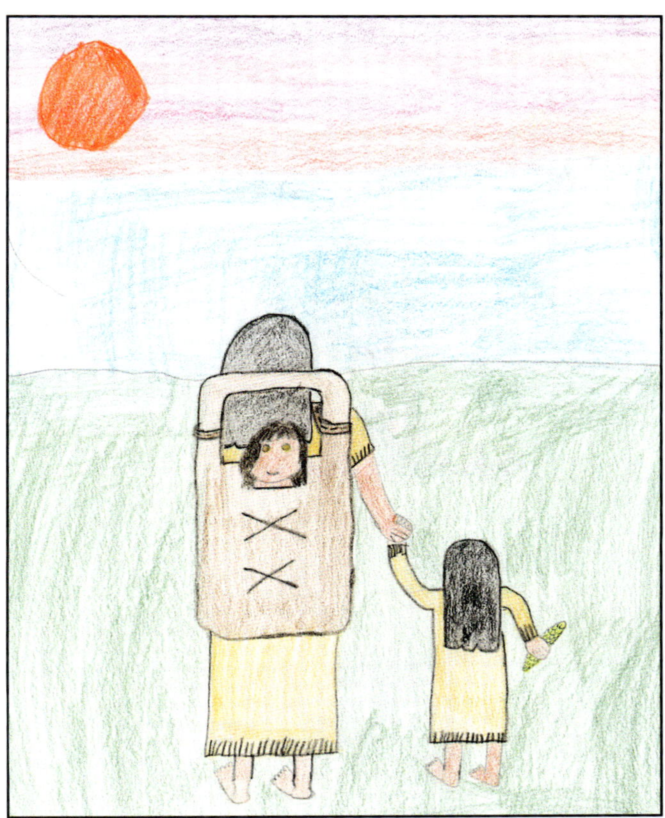

Mother and Children by Hannah Fyne, age 9
from Draw•Write•Now®, Book Three

5. Color the Picture

Children enjoy coloring their own drawings. The beautiful colors, however, often cover the details they have so carefully drawn in pencil. To preserve their efforts, you may want to have the children trace their pencil lines with black crayons or fine-tipped felt markers.

Crayons—When coloring with crayons, have the children outline their drawings with a black crayon *after* they have colored their pictures (the black crayon may smear if they do their outlining first).

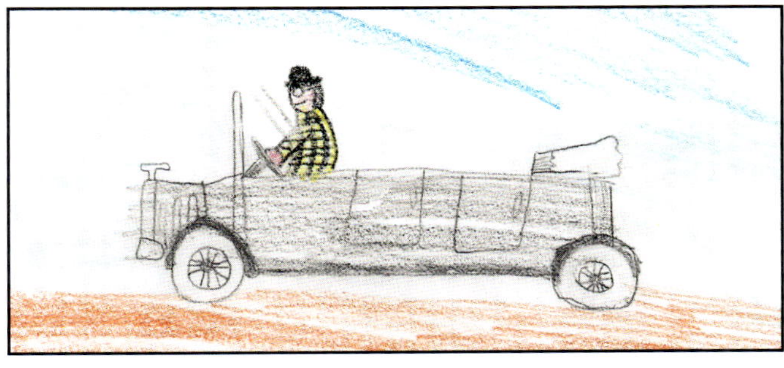

Model T by Charlotte Morrison, age 6
from Draw•Write•Now®, Book Five

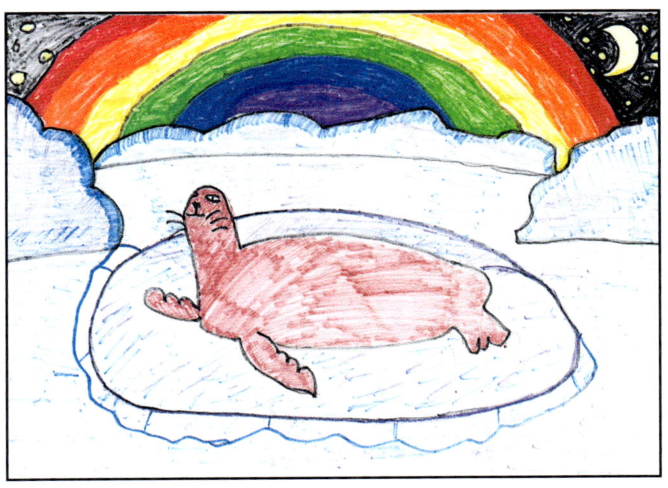

Seal by Kevin Brown, age 8
from Draw•Write•Now®, Book Four

Color Pencils—When coloring with color pencils, have the children outline their drawings with a felt tip marker *before* they color their drawings.

Felt Tip Markers—When coloring with felt tip markers, have the children outline their drawings with a black marker *after* they have colored their pictures.

Your comments are appreciated!

*How are you sharing **Draw•Write•Now®** with your children or students? The authors would appreciate hearing from you. Write to Kim Stitzer, c/o Rainbow Resource Center, Inc., 655 Township Rd 500E, Toulon, IL 61483, USA or visit www.rainbowresource.com.*

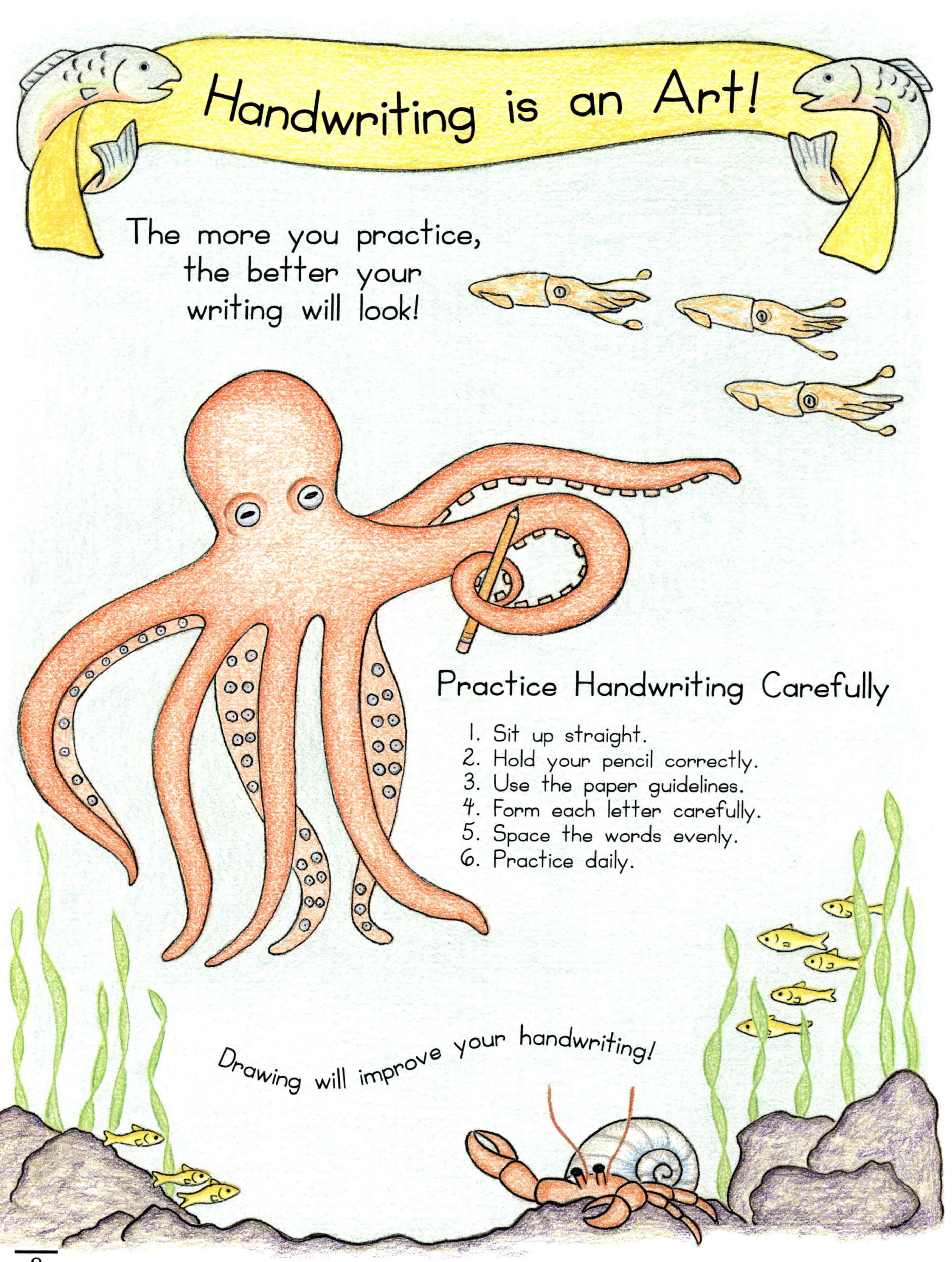
Handwriting is an Art!
The more you practice,
the better your
writing will look!
Practice Handwriting Carefully
1. Sit up straight.
2. Hold your pencil correctly.
3. Use the paper guidelines.
4. Form each letter carefully.
5. Space the words evenly.
6. Practice daily.
Drawing will improve your handwriting!

On Land

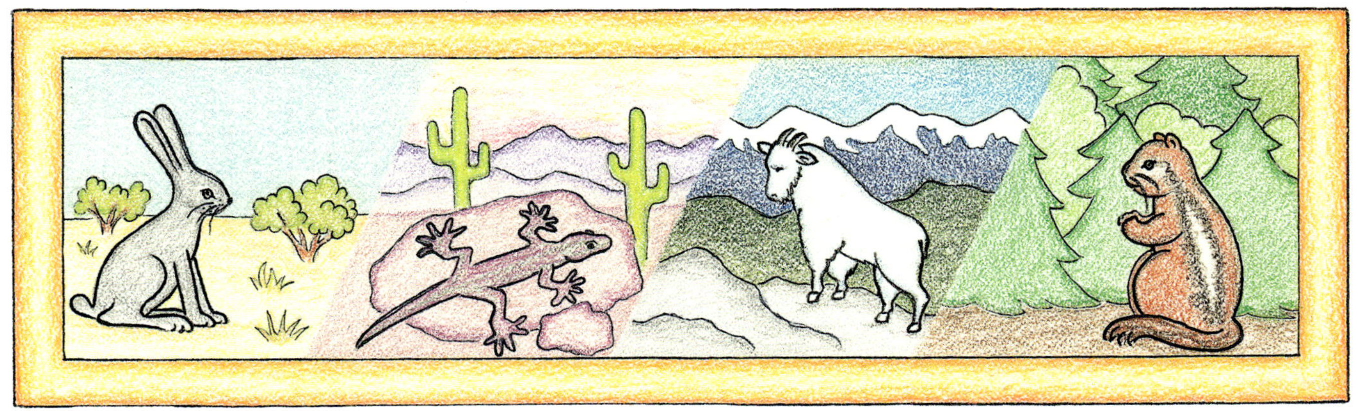

Land Animals

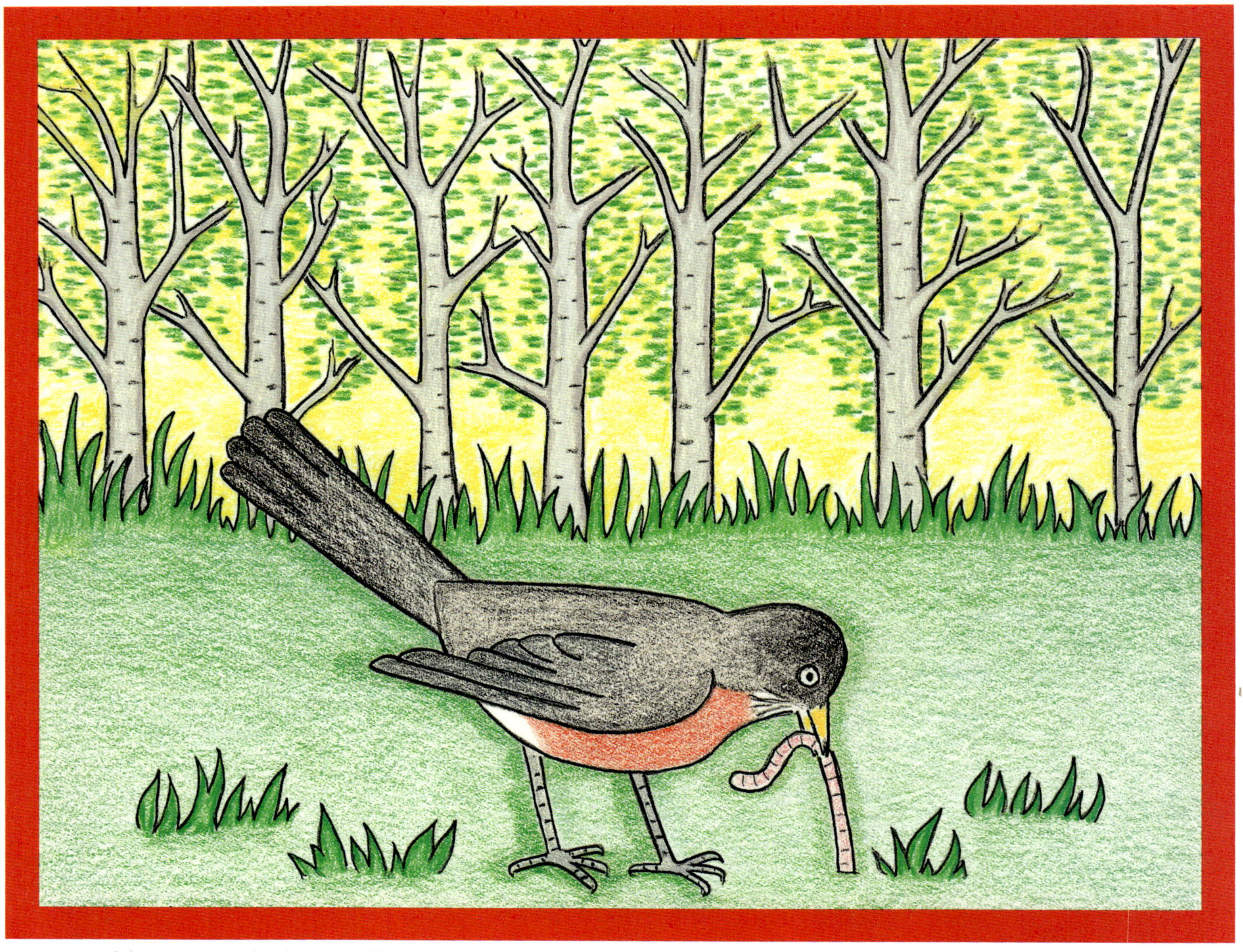

Land homes include woodlands, grasslands, shrub lands, dry lands, mountains and lowlands.

The ground is land.
Plants grow out of the ground.
Many animals live on land.
Even birds need land.

Are earthworms animals?

Land Homes

Teaching Tip on page 64
Question answered on page 32

Robin

1.

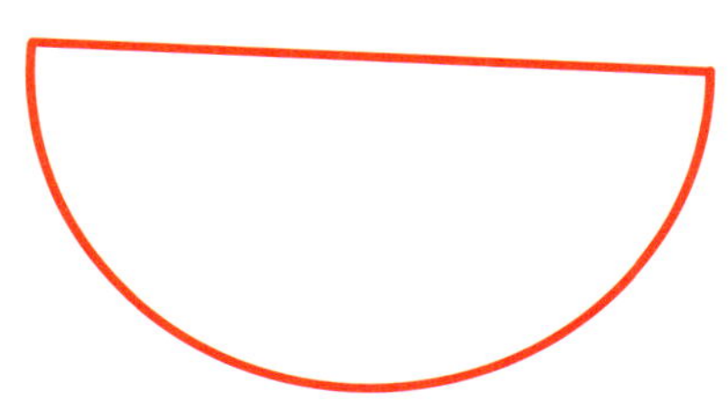

2.

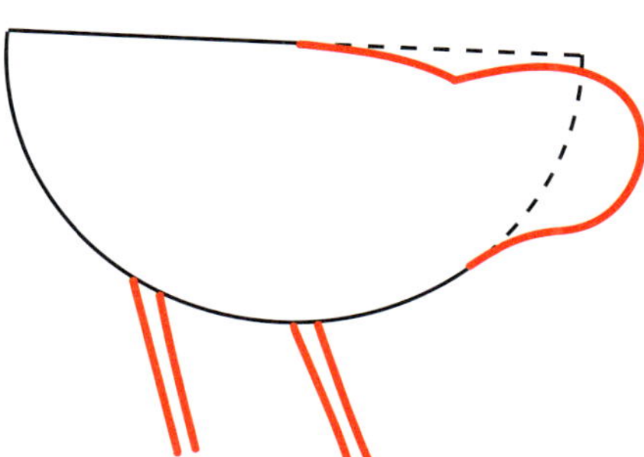

3.

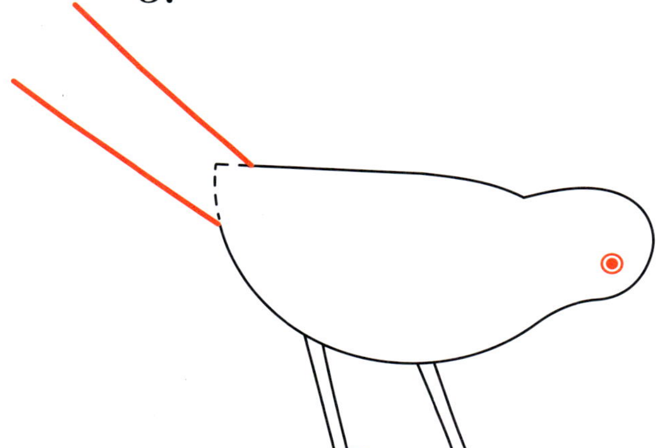

4.

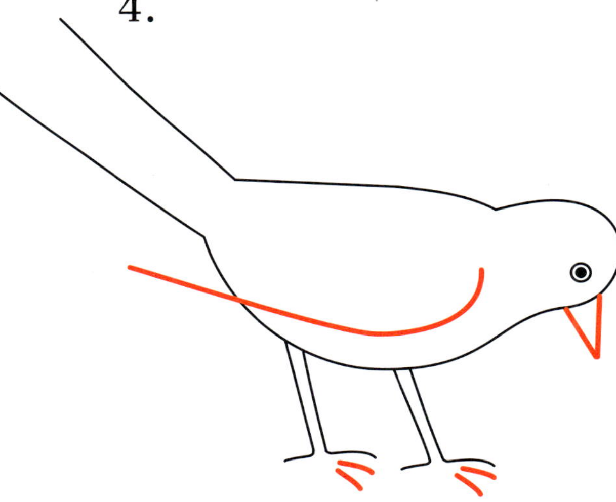

5.

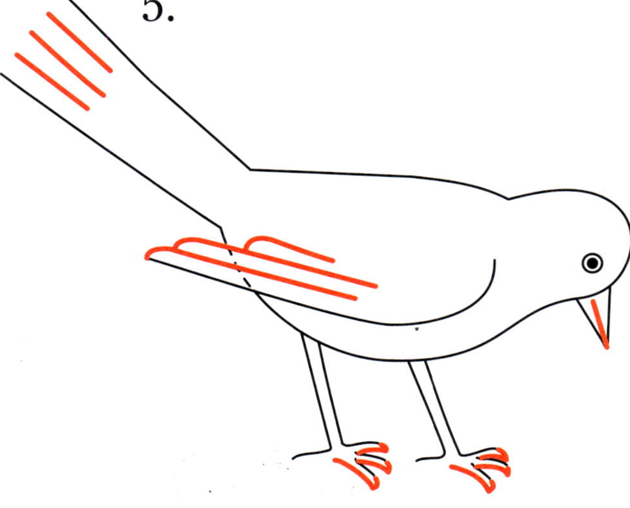

6.

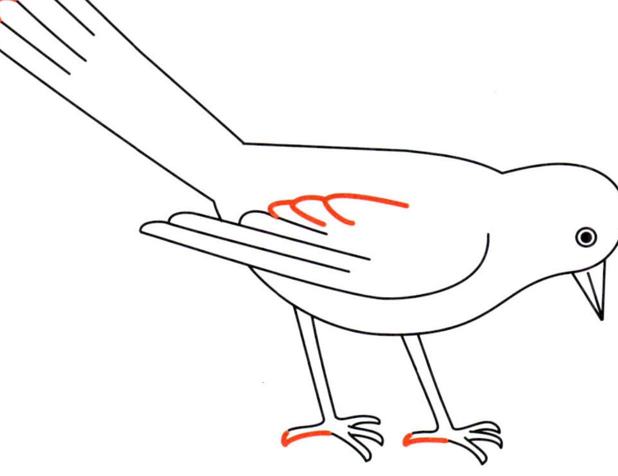

Woodlands

Question answered on page 26

Chipmunk

1.

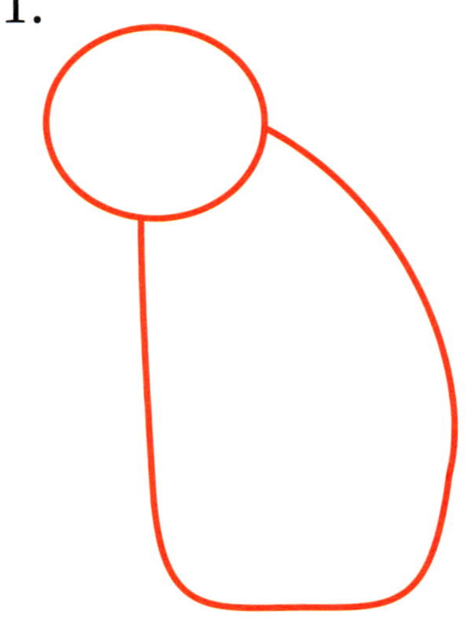

2.

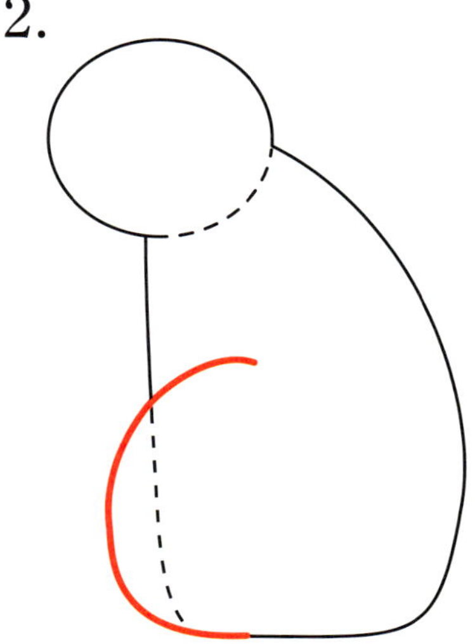

3.

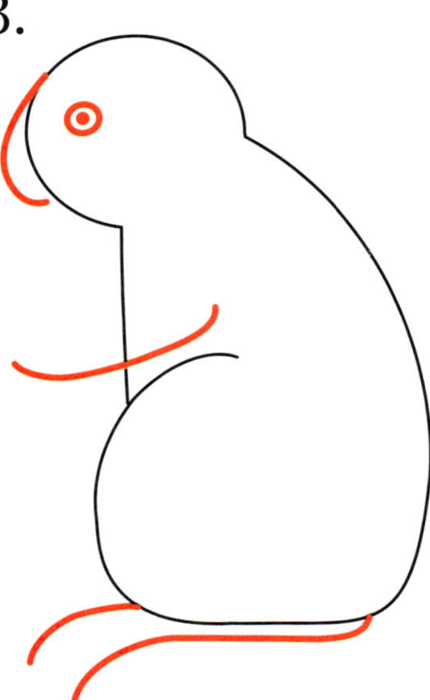

4.

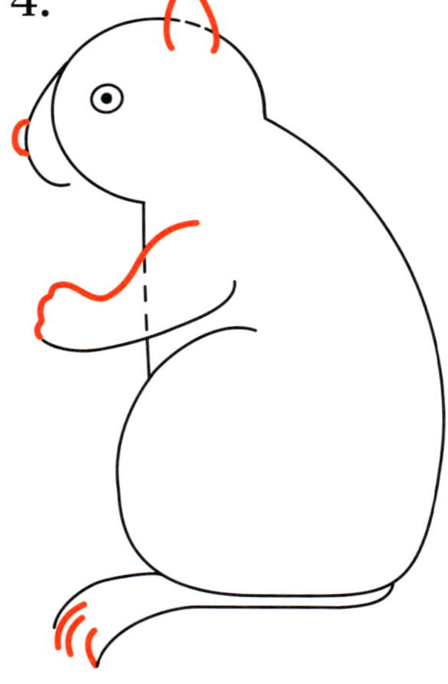

5.

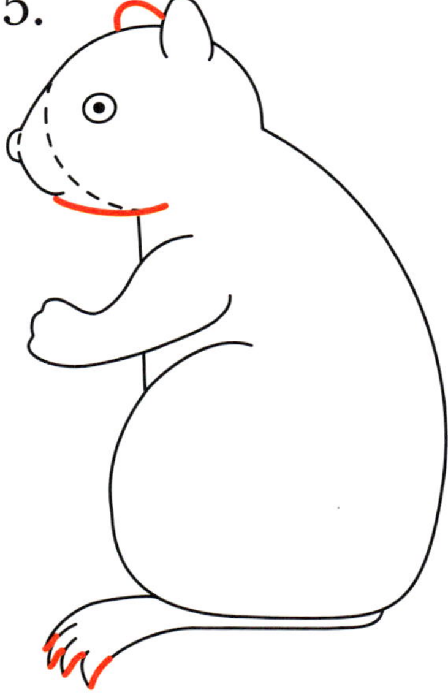

6.

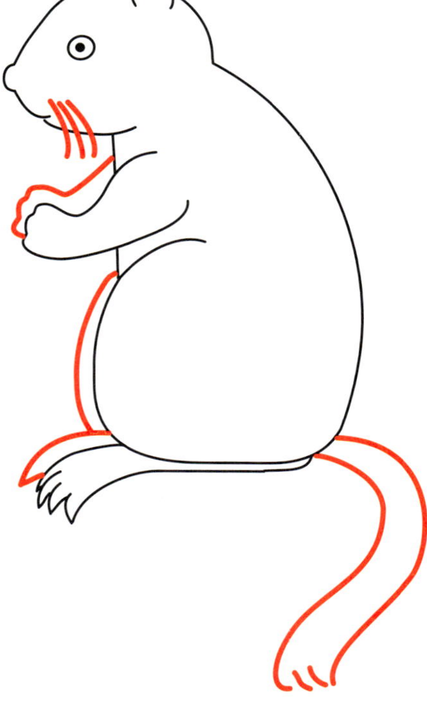

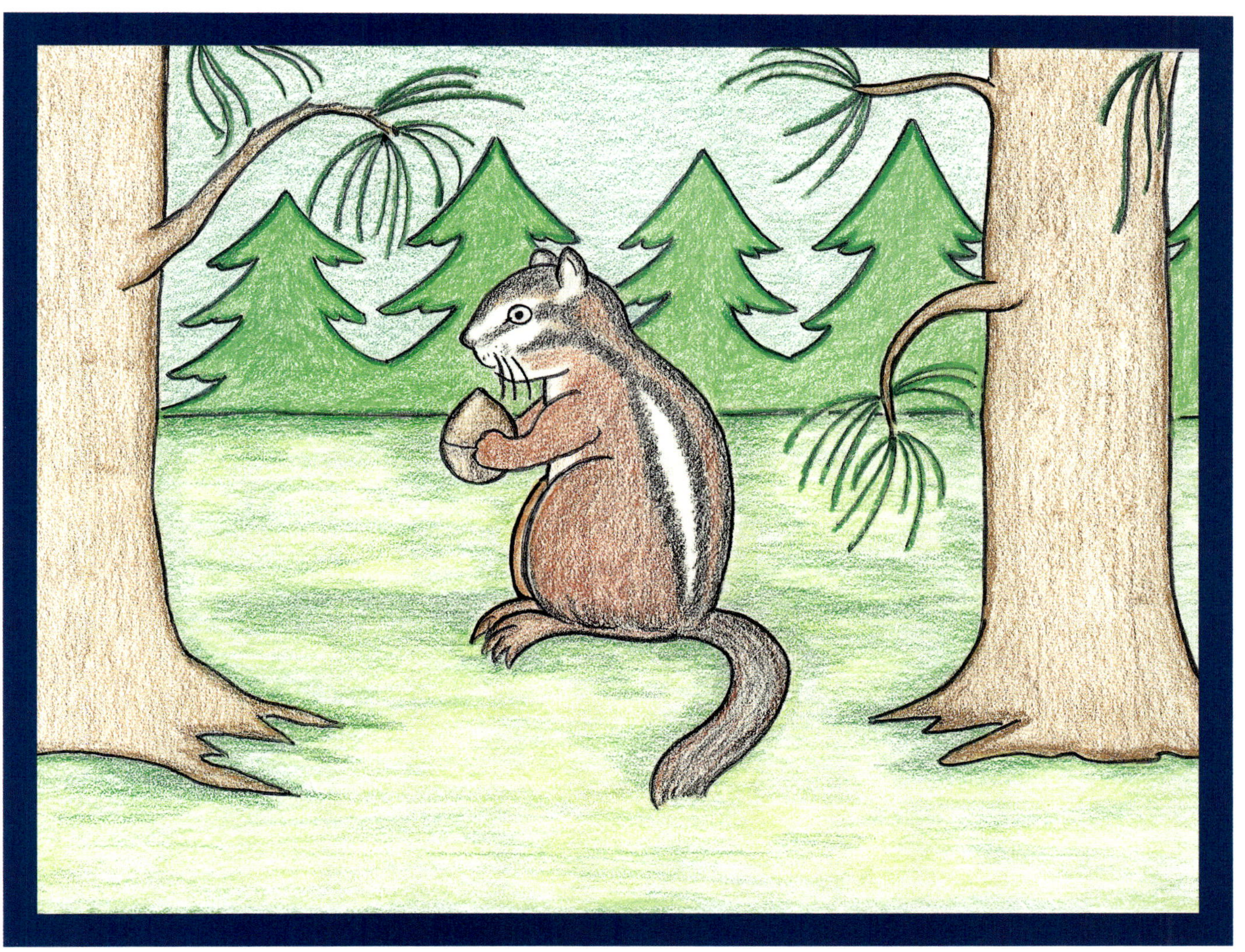

Woodlands include forests, rainforests, jungles and taigas.

Trees grow in woodlands.
Many animals live among trees.
Some nest on branches.
Chipmunks sleep underground.

Where is the best animal home?

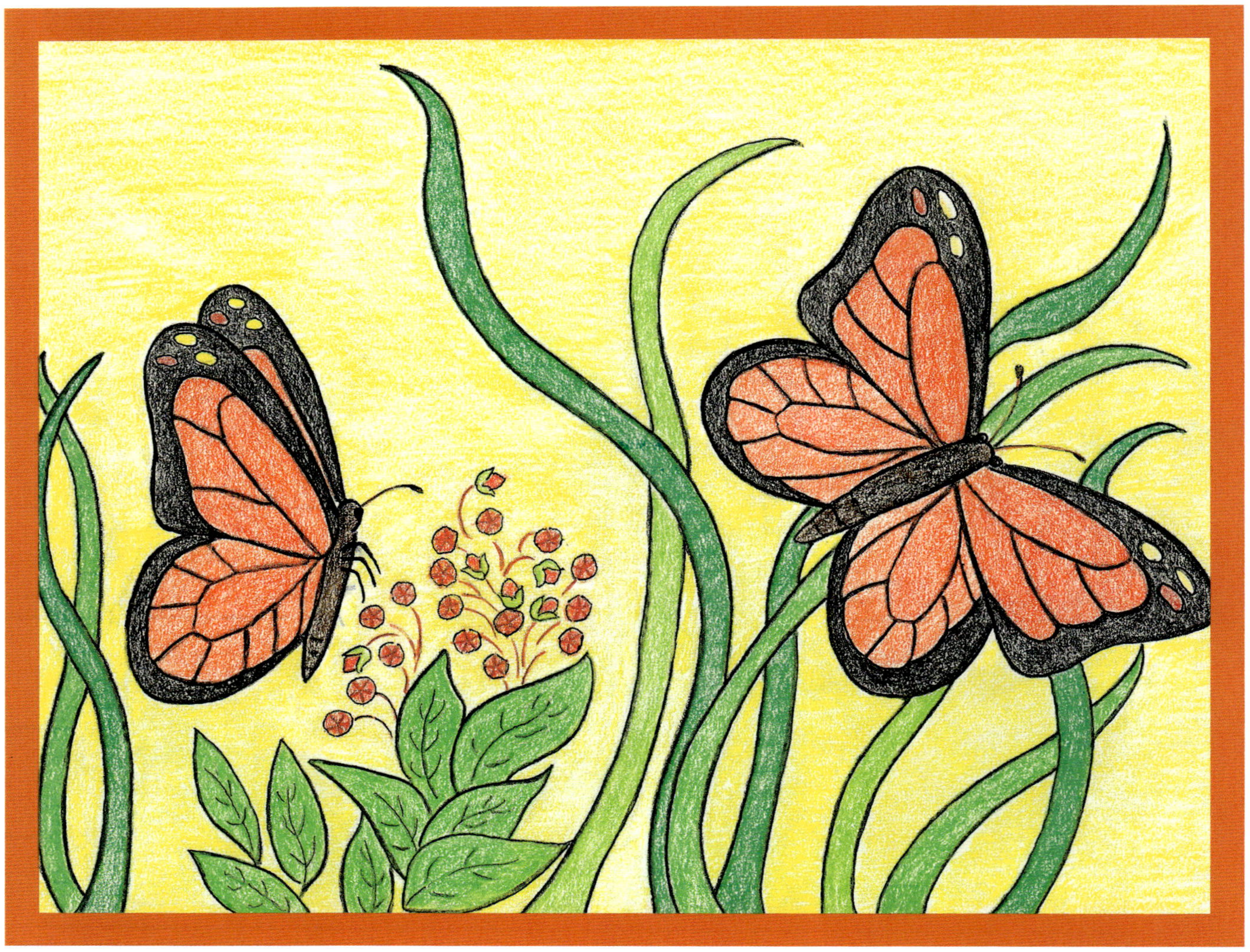

Grasslands include prairies, meadows, fields, plains, savannahs, pampas and steppes.

Many insects live in grasslands.
Small plants provide food.
Caterpillars live on the plants.
Some become butterflies.

Where do butterflies go when it rains?

Monarch eggs

Young monarch caterpillars

Monarch chrysalis

Question answered on page 26

Monarch Butterfly

1.

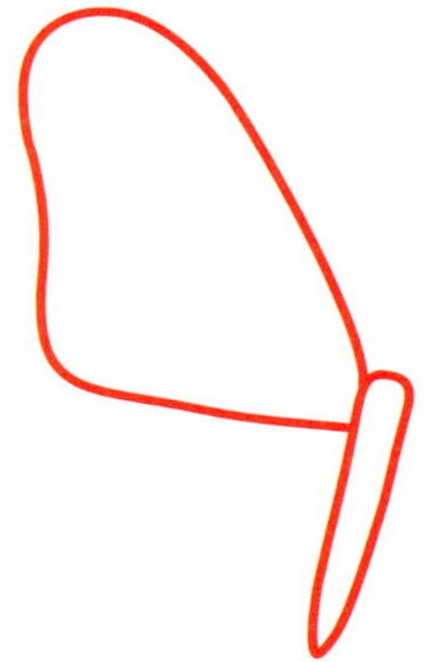

2.

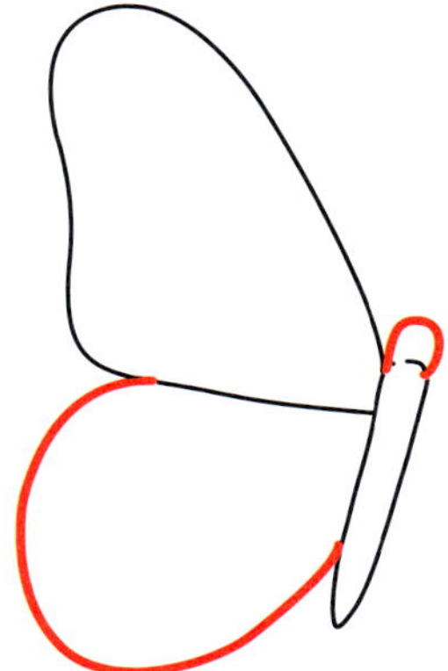

3.

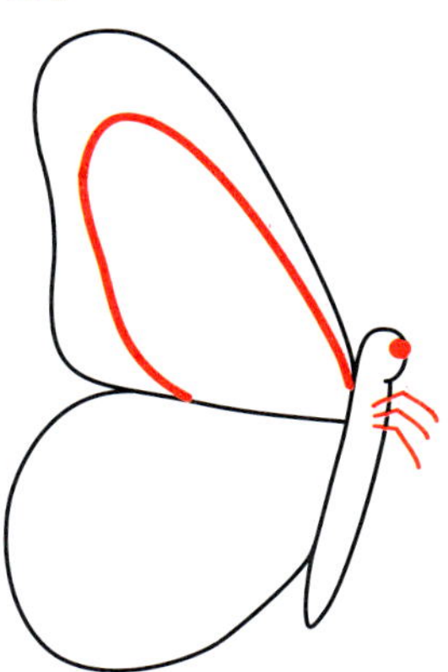

4.

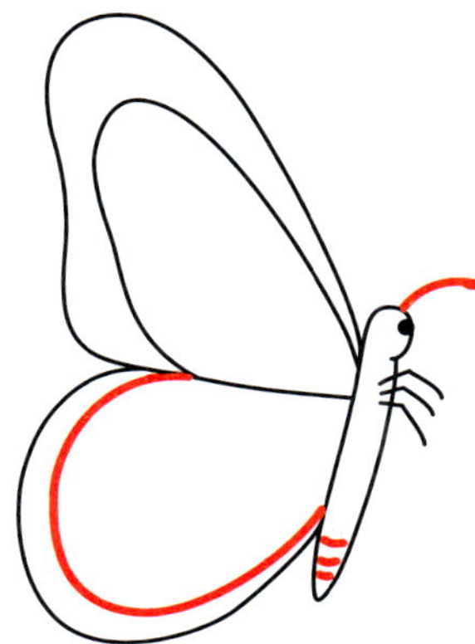

5.

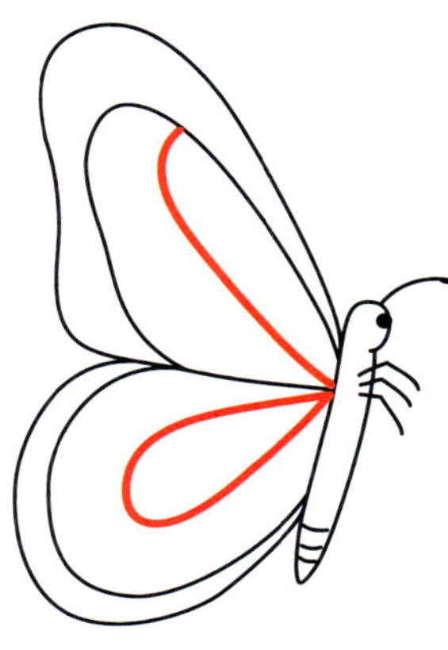

6.

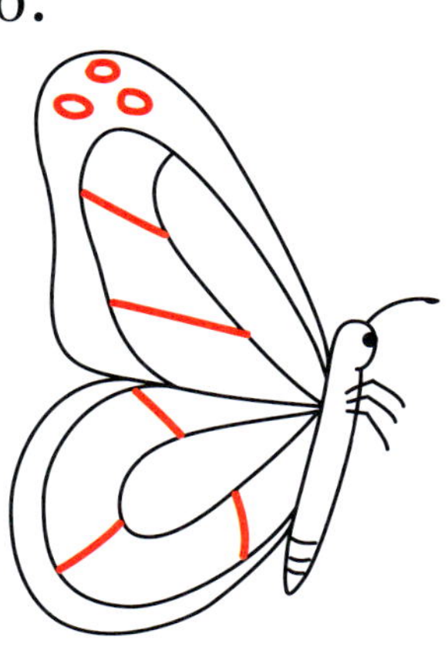

7.

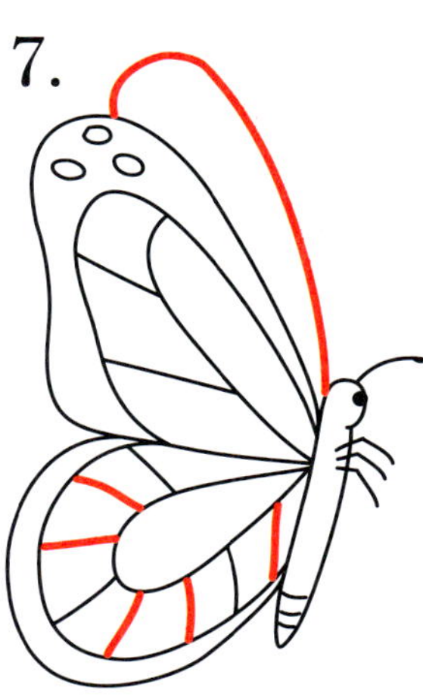

8.

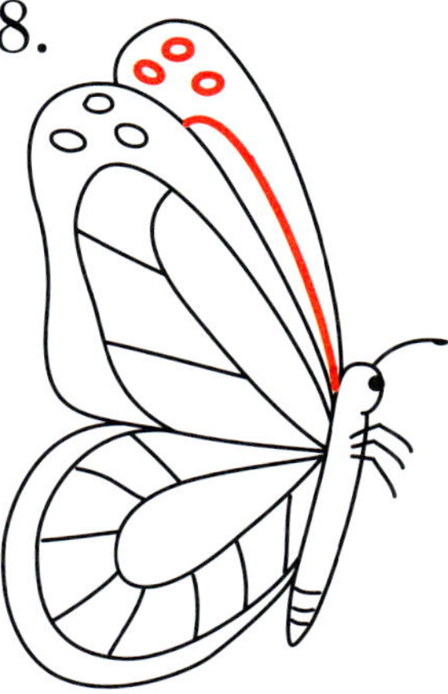

1.

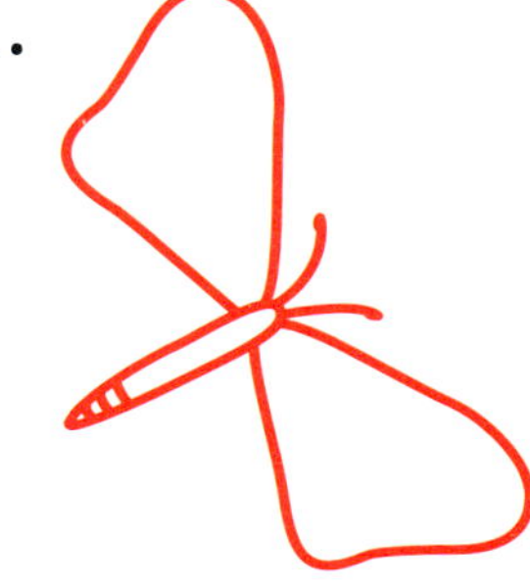

2.

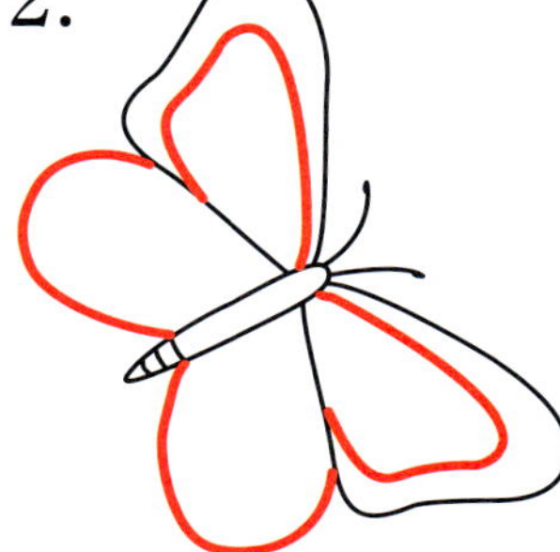

3.

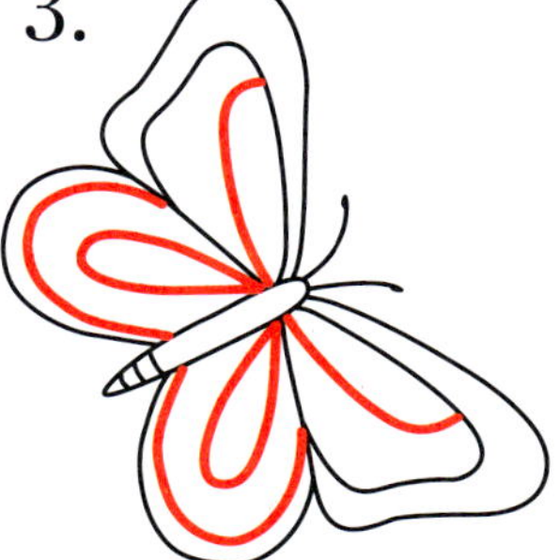

4.

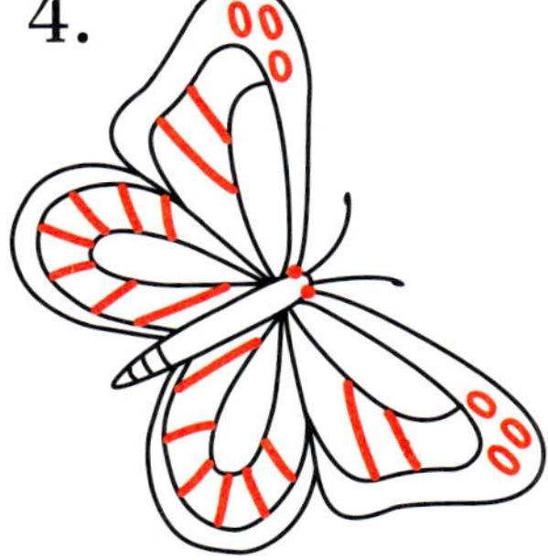

Shrub Lands

Teaching Tip on page 64
Question answered on page 26

Jackrabbit

1.

2.

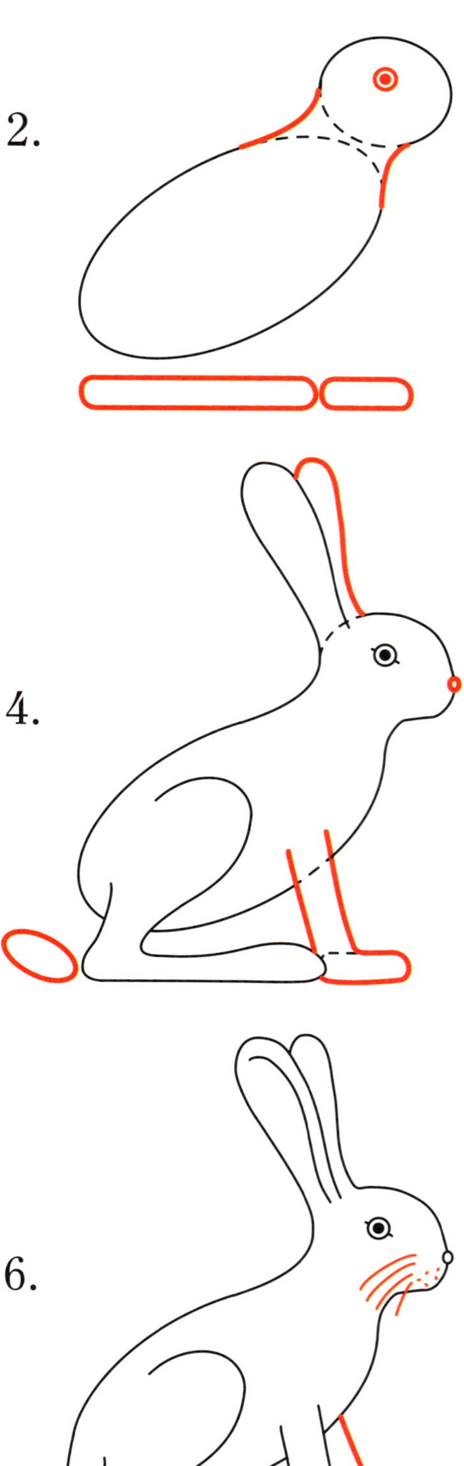

3.

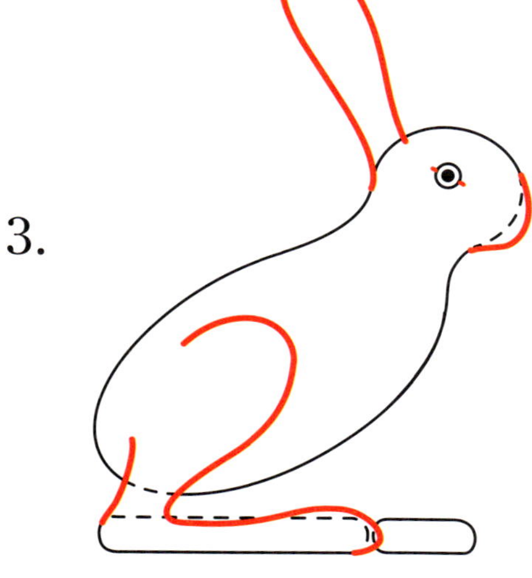

4.

5.

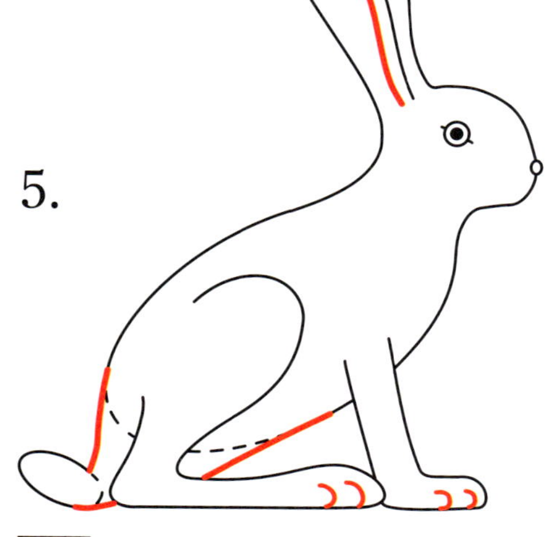

6.

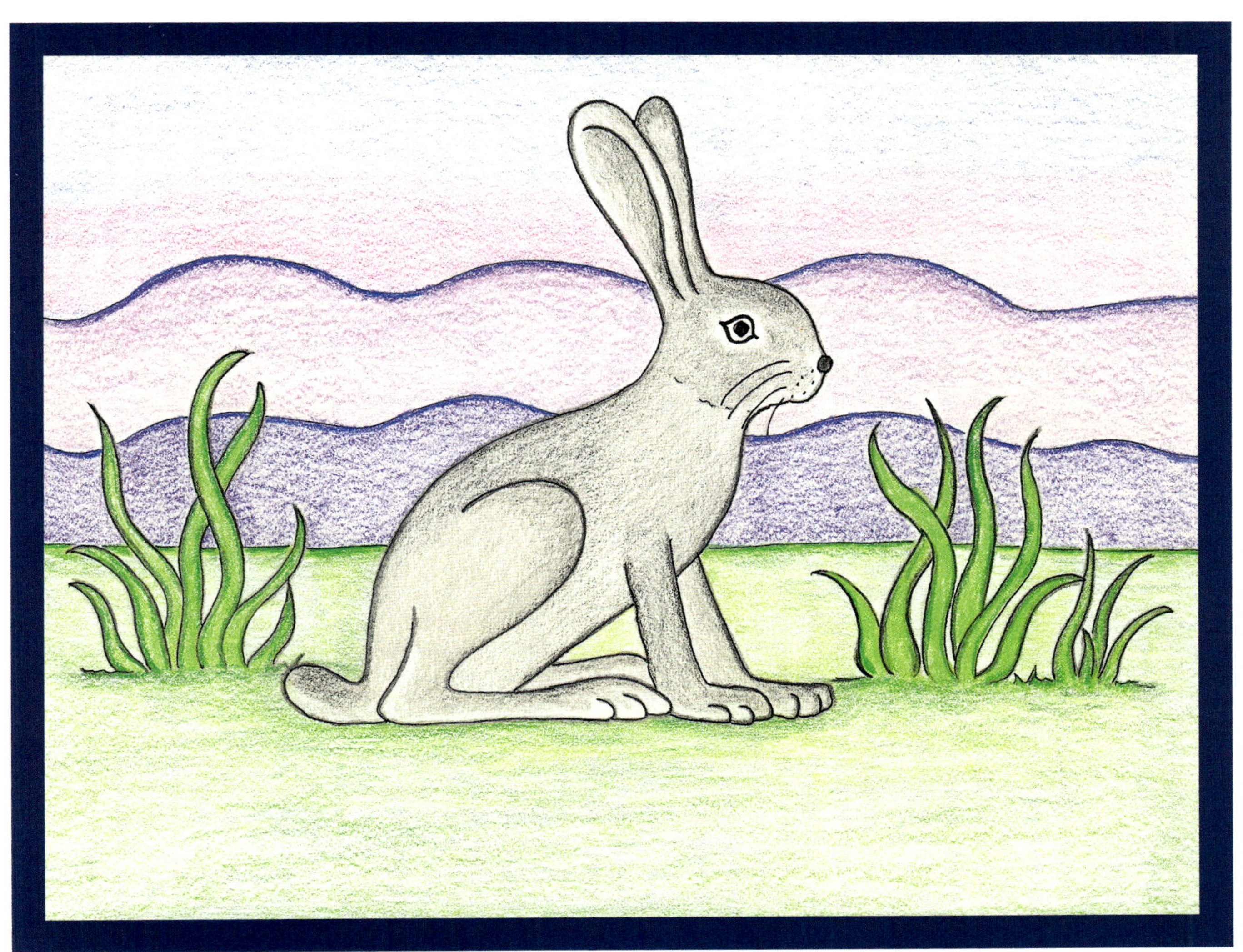

Shrub lands include chaparrals, caatingas and mallees.

Jackrabbits live in shrub lands.
They hop away from danger.
Summers are long and dry.
The plants have small leaves.

Are bushes the only plants that grow in shrub lands?

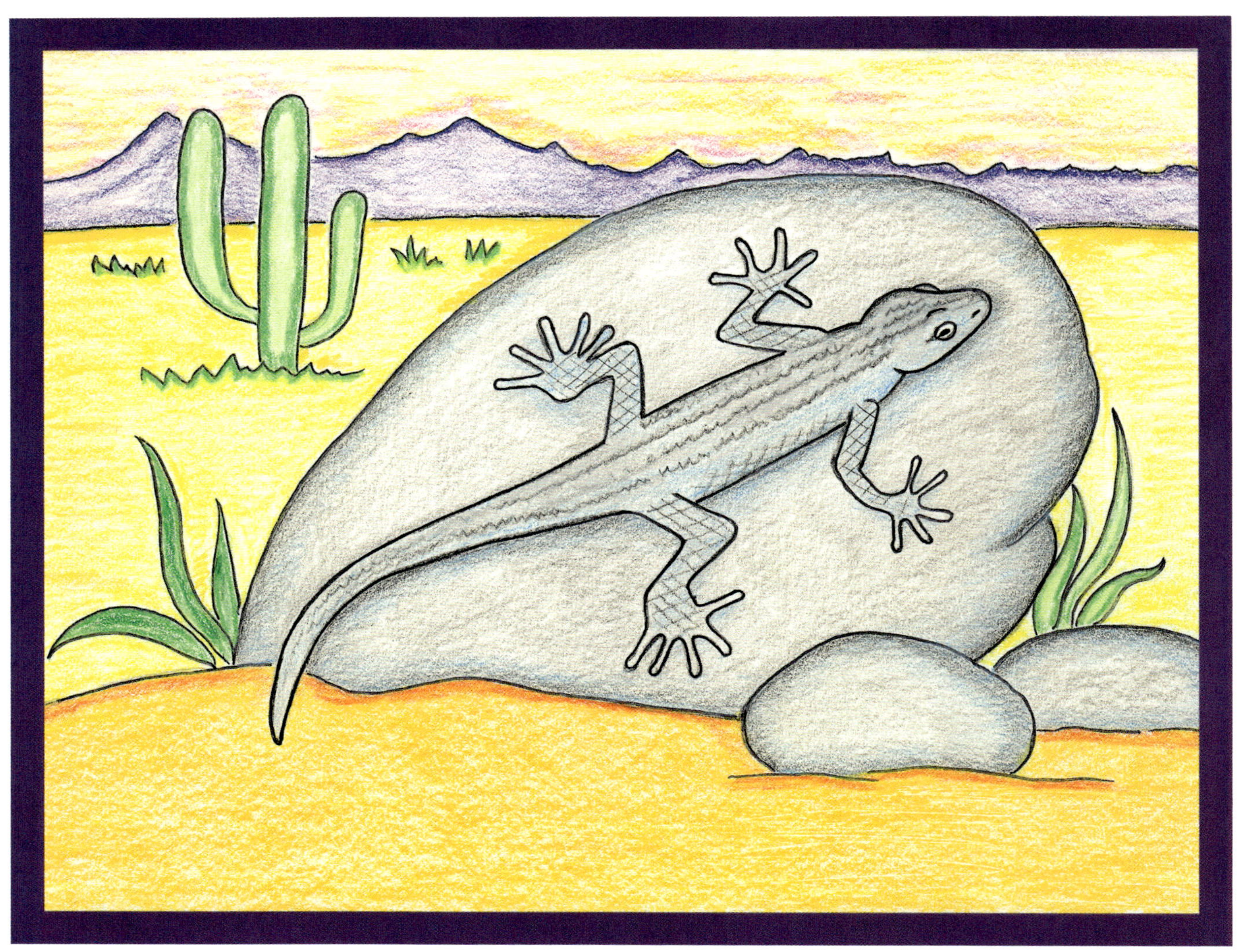

Dry lands include deserts, sagebrush lands, scrub lands and brush lands.

Some places are very dry.
Dry land plants need little water.
Lizards warm up in the sunshine.
They cool off in the shade.

Are all dry lands hot?

Dry Lands

Question answered on page 26

Lizard

1.

2.

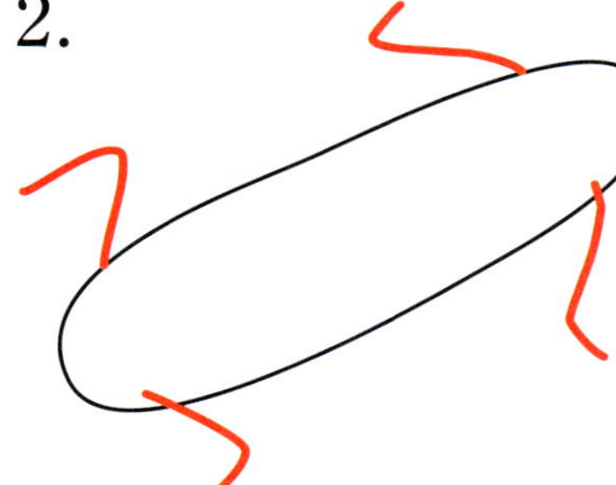

3.

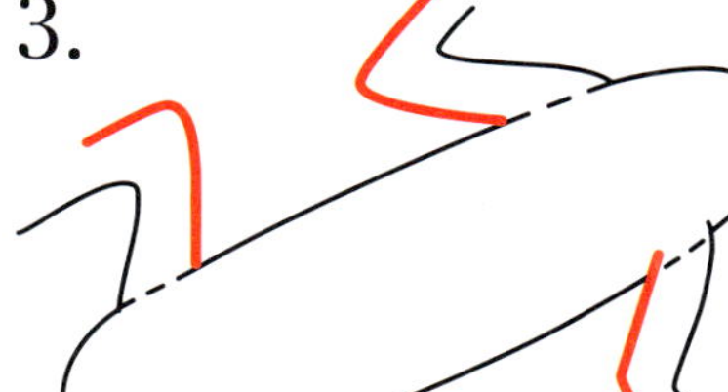

4.

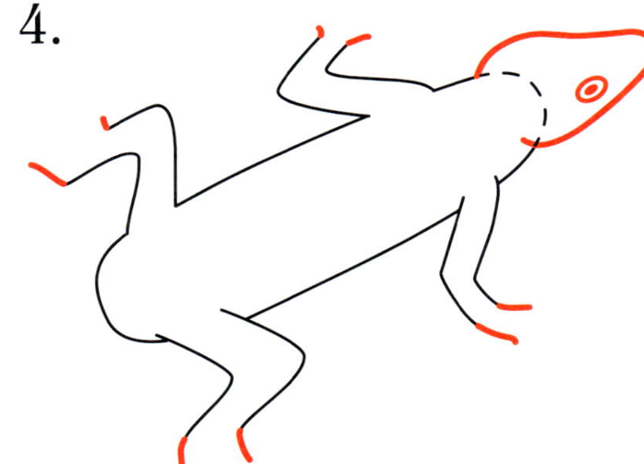

5.

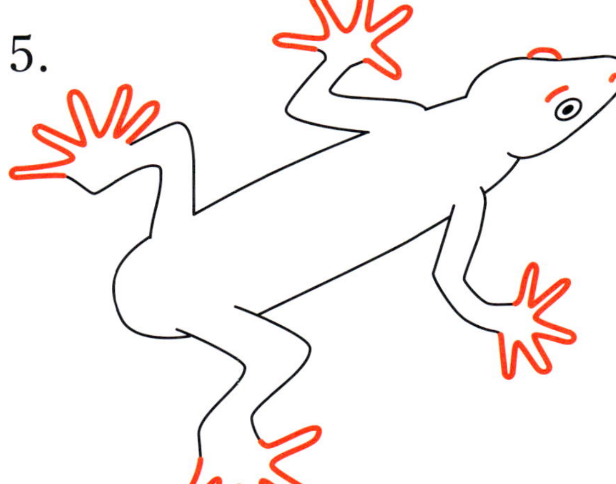

6.

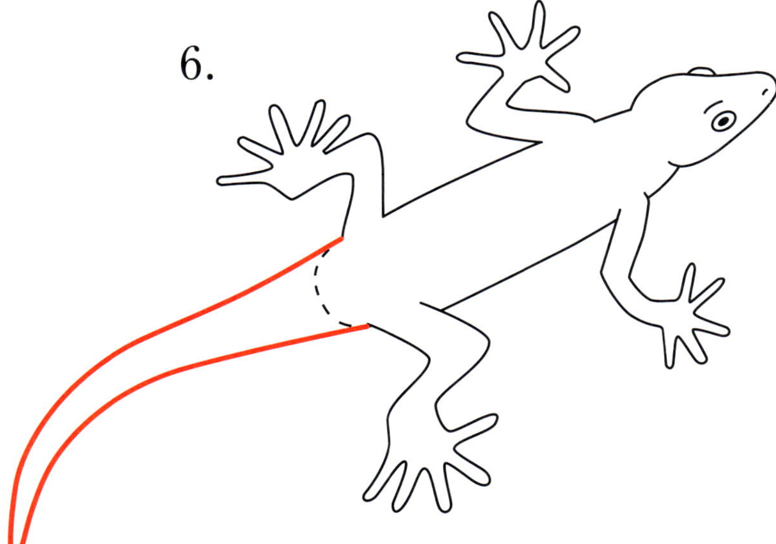

Mountains

Teaching Tip on page 64
Question answered on page 26

Mountain Goat

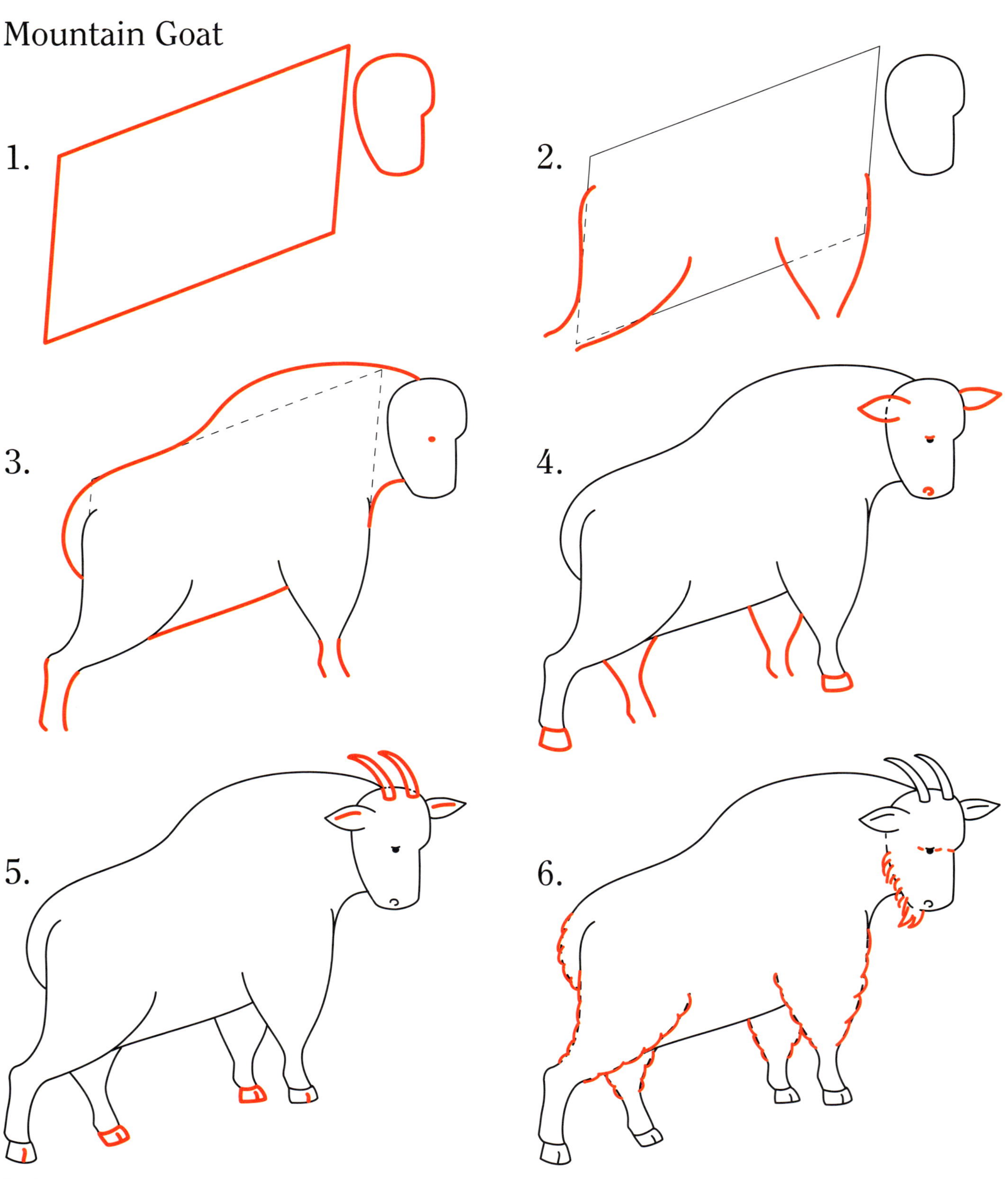

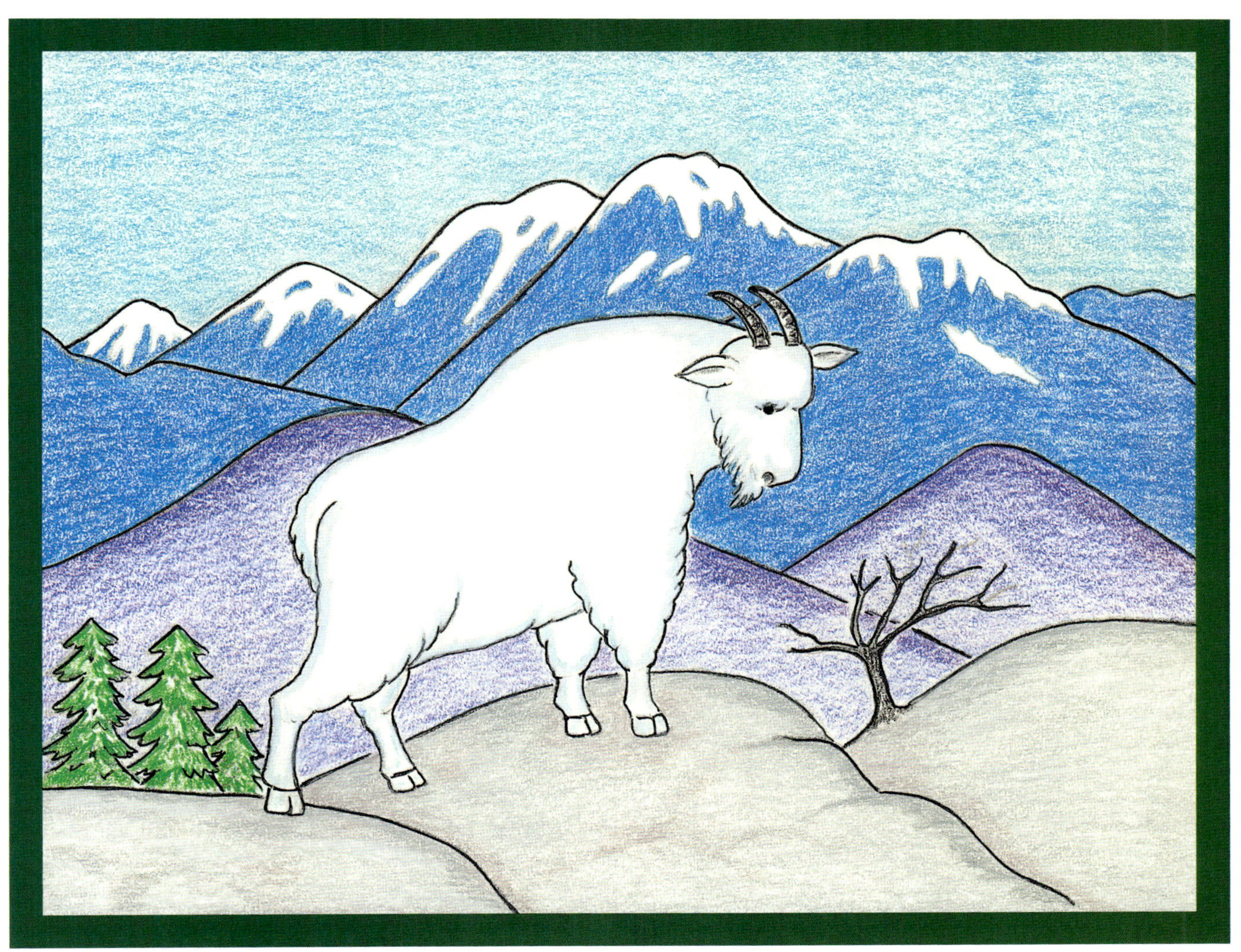

Mountain ranges include snow-capped peaks and alpine tundras.

The highest lands are mountains.
The air has little oxygen.
Mountain goats climb the peaks.
They see far away.

How are mountains, the Arctic and the Antarctic alike?

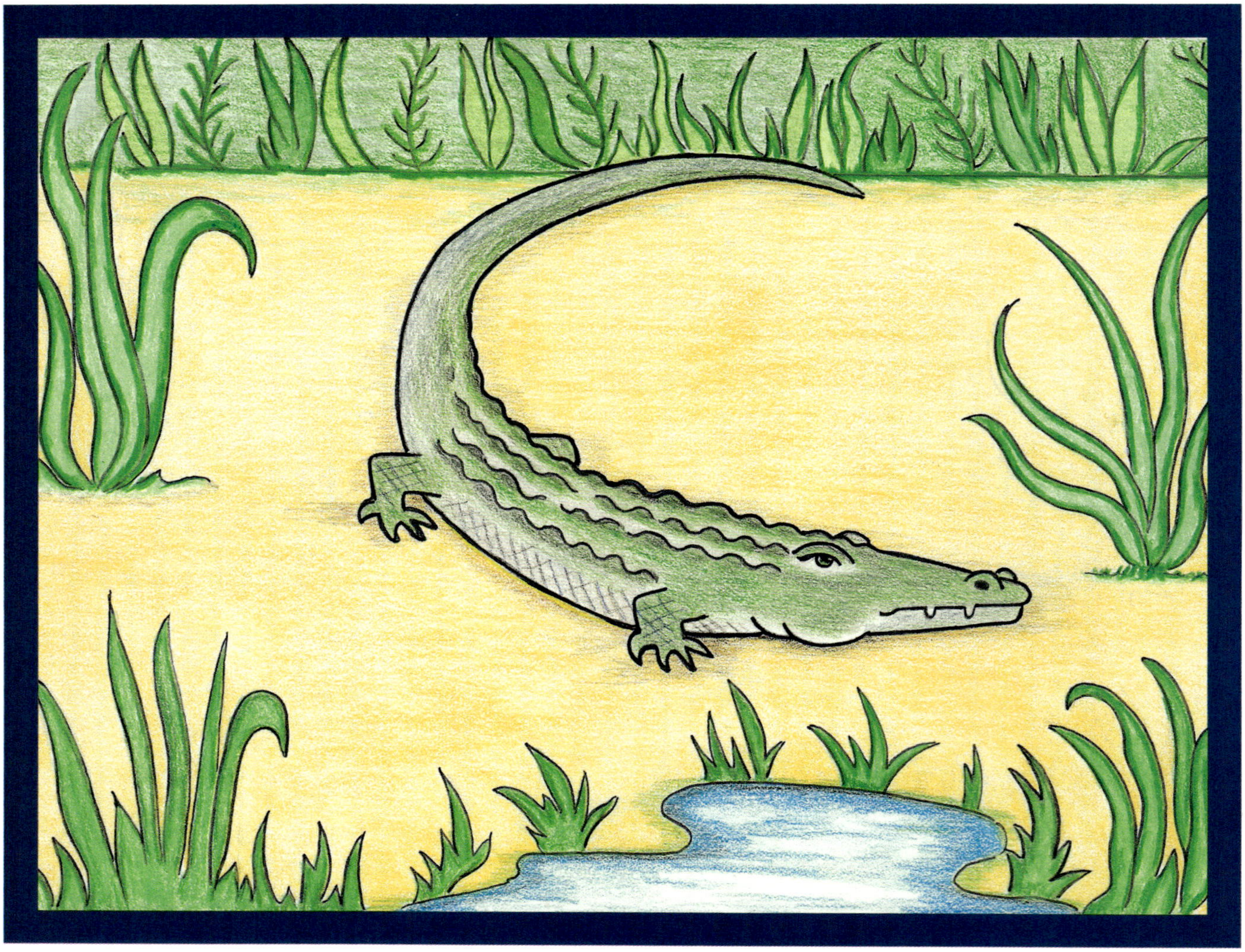

Lowlands include coastal lands.

Most lowlands are by oceans.
This land is near sea level.
Crocodiles need to be by water.
They hide in the water.

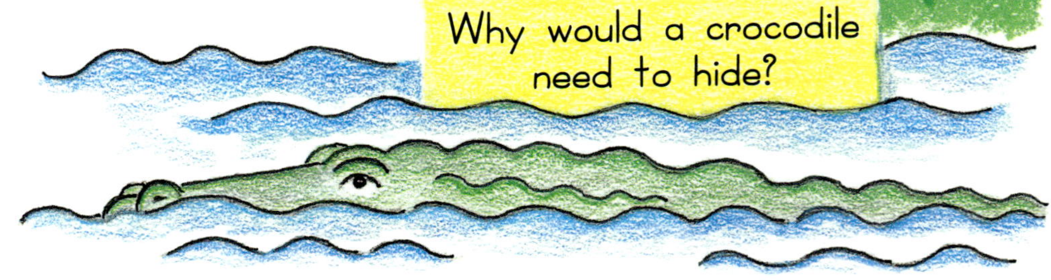

Question answered on page 26

Crocodile

1.

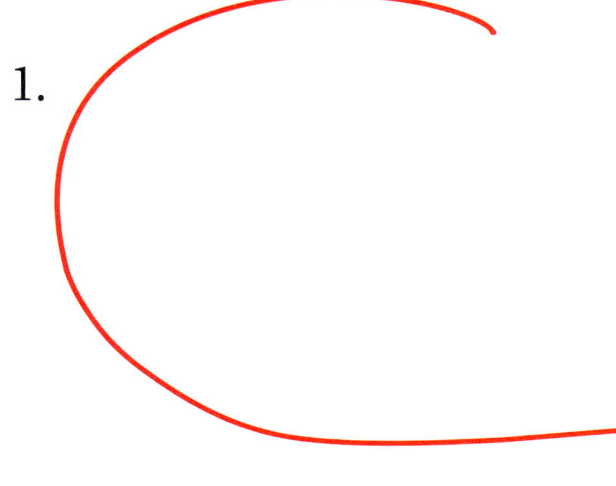

2.

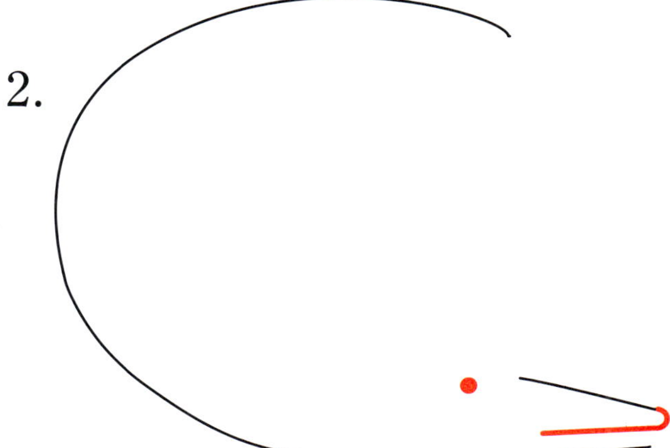

3.

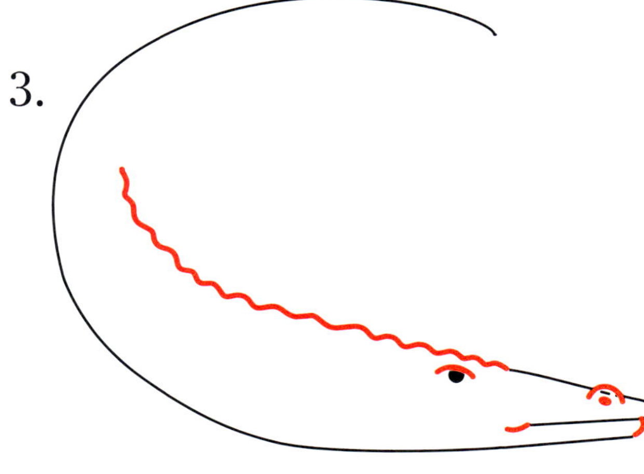

4.

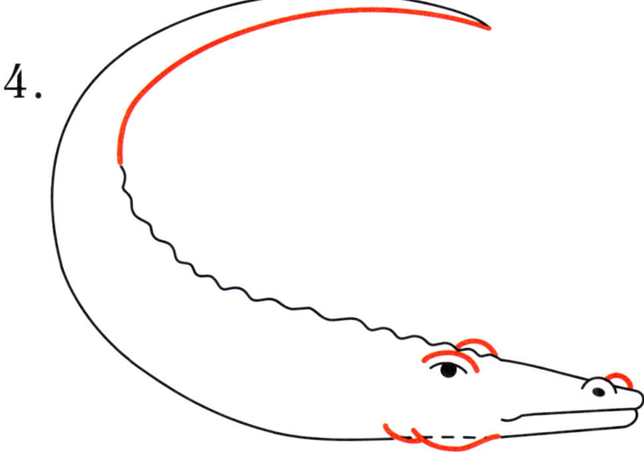

5.

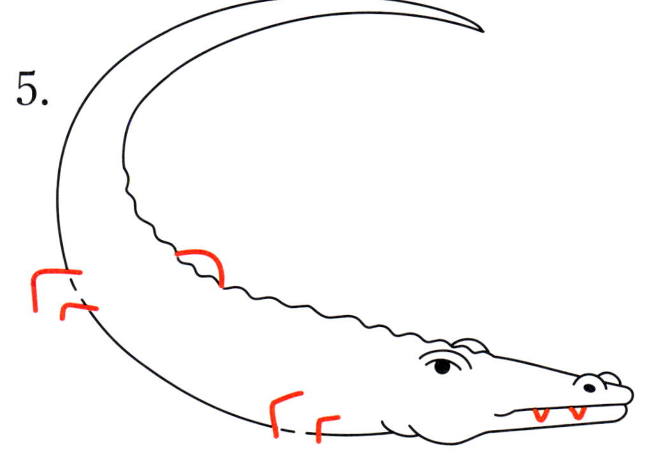

6.

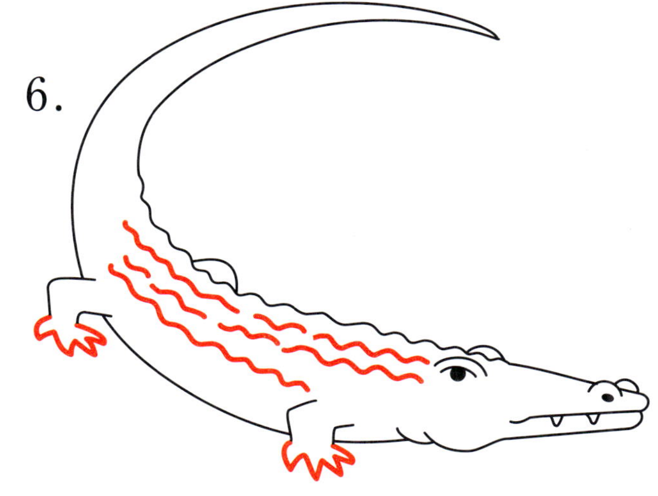

Draw What You See

Where do you live? Visit natural habitats near your home. What do you see?

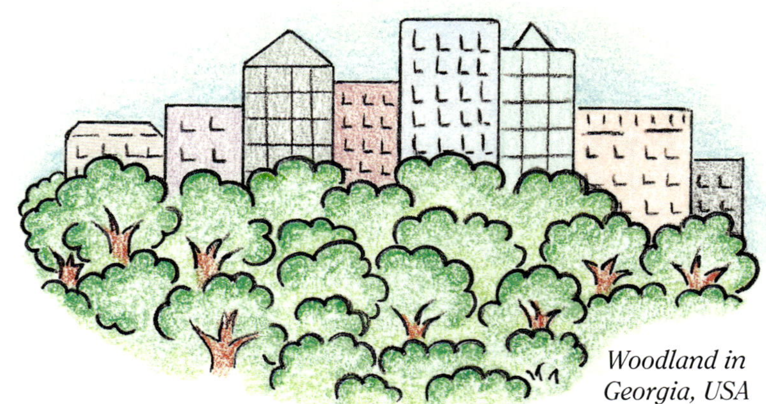

Woodland in Georgia, USA

A place with many trees

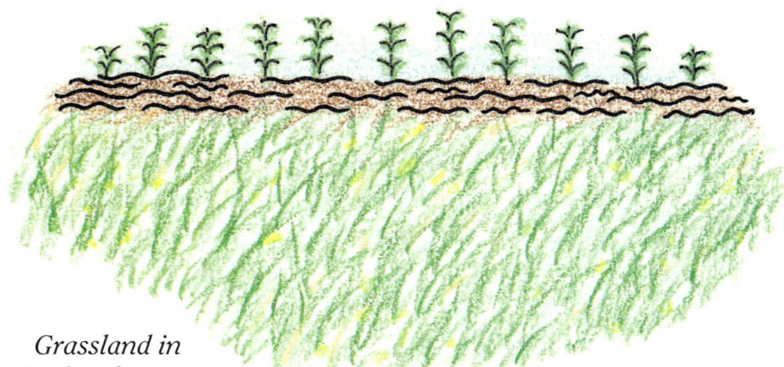

Grassland in Saskatchewan, Canada

A place with mostly grasses and wild flowers

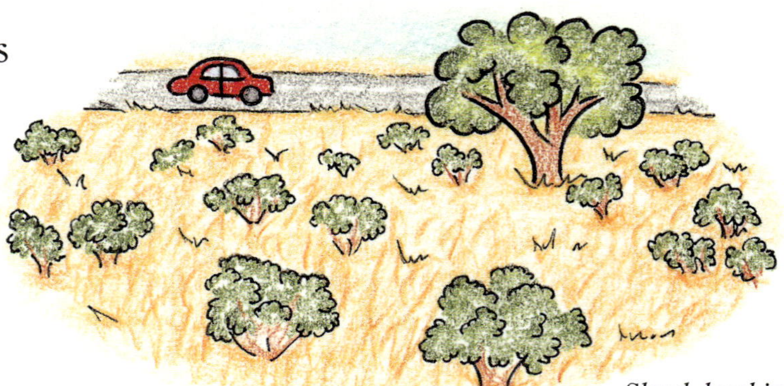

Shrub land in California, USA

A place with bushes and low trees

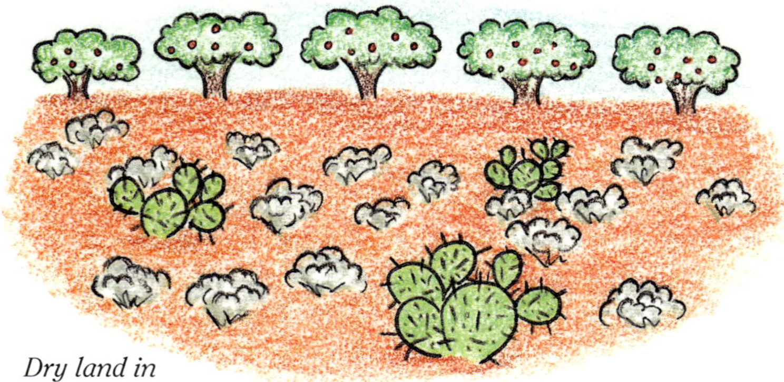

Dry land in Mexico

A place of sand, rock or clay, and tough plants

What is the horizon line?

Look outside.
The place where the sky and earth meet is called the horizon line.

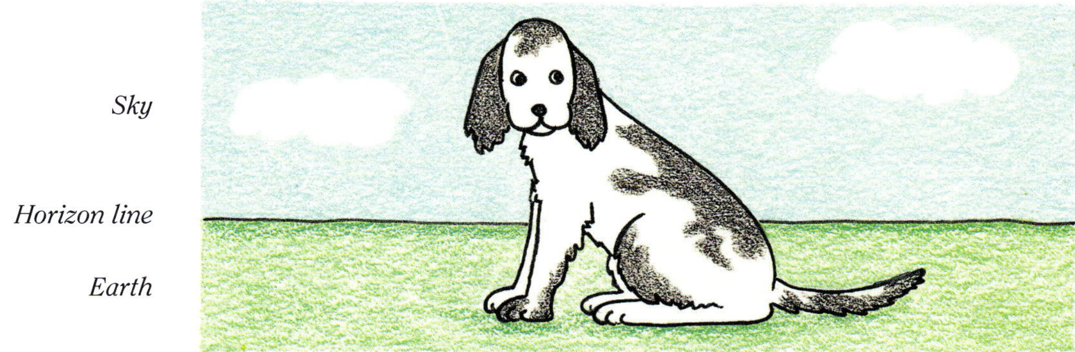

Look inside.
Pretend the wall is the sky and the floor is the earth. The baseboard is the horizon line.

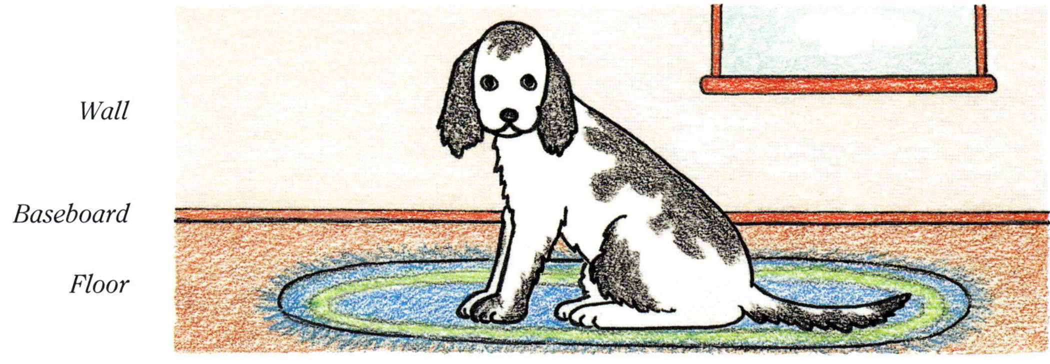

Plants, buildings and mountains can make the horizon line hard to see!

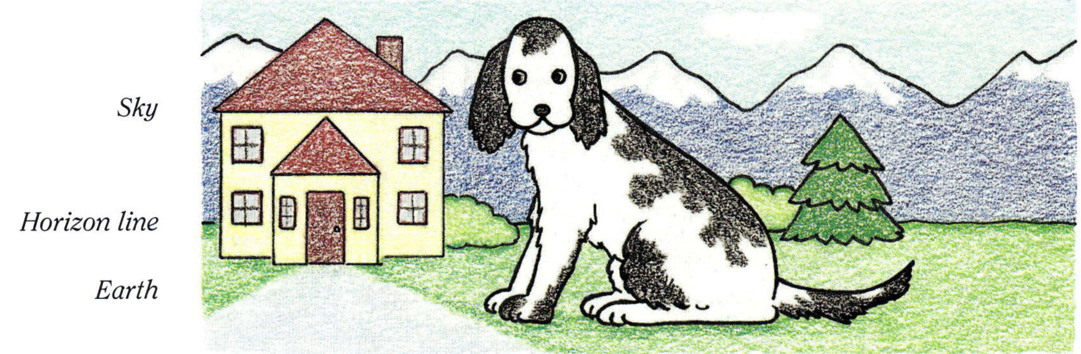

Learn more about land habitats...

ARE EARTHWORMS ANIMALS? PAGE 10

Yes, earthworms are animals. Try classifying the animals, plants and land shown in ANIMAL, VEGETABLE, MINERAL? *photographed by Tana Hoban, published by Greenwillow, 1995. (Here's a little help! Sponges are animals.) Then, learn about Earth's renewable resources with* YOU'RE ABOARD SPACESHIP EARTH *by Patricia Lauber, illustrated by Holly Keller, published by HarperCollins, 1996.*

WHERE IS THE BEST ANIMAL HOME? Page 13

Earth has a variety of places for animals to call home. The best home for each animal is the place where it feels most comfortable. A boy and mother realize this in THE SALAMANDER ROOM *by Anne Mazer, illustrated by Steve Johnson, published by Knopf, 1991. A home beneath the ground is perfect for some animals. See* CHIPMUNK SONG *by Joanne Ryder, illustrated by Lynne Cherry, published by Puffin Unicorn, 1987. Then, enter the shelter of bushes in* RABBITS & RAINDROPS *written and illustrated by Jim Arnosky, published by Putnam, 1997. Some animals choose manmade environments, like the birds in* URBAN ROOSTS *written and illustrated by Barbara Bash, published by Sierra Club, 1990.*

WHERE DO BUTTERFLIES GO WHEN IT RAINS? Page 14

Butterflies find shelter in trees and other plants when it rains. Learn how important grassland plants are to the monarch butterfly with AN EXTRAORDINARY LIFE *by Laurence Pringle, illustrated by Bob Marstall, published by Orchard, 1997. Few trees can grow in a grassland because there is not enough rainfall. See a grassland in great need of rain in* BRINGING THE RAIN TO KAPITI PLAIN *by Verna Aardema, illustrated by Beatriz Vidal, published by Dial, 1981.*

ARE BUSHES THE ONLY PLANTS THAT GROW IN SHRUB LANDS? Page 17

Along with bushes or shrubs, plants with deep roots and trees with small, tough leaves also grow in shrub lands. In North America, much of the state of California is shrub land. Read the story of an orphaned jackrabbit who is raised by caring people in northern California, then returned to the wild in JACKRABBIT *by Jonathan London, illustrated by Deborah Kogan Ray, published by Crown, 1996.*

ARE ALL DRY LANDS HOT? Page 18

Most dry lands are hot, but there are exceptions. In high elevations and the polar regions, deserts and scrub lands are cold places. There is even a desert in Antarctica! Experience the unique colors of the arid landscape with WELCOME TO THE SEA OF SAND *by Jane Yolen, illustrated by Laura Regan, published by Putnam's Sons, 1996.*

Lizards may be red or green, stripped or dotted. See how color protects animals with WHAT COLOR IS CAMOUFLAGE? *by Carolyn Otto, illustrated by Megan Lloyd, published by HarperCollins, 1996.*

HOW ARE MOUNTAINS, THE ARCTIC AND THE ANTARCTIC ALIKE? Page 21

Both have long cold seasons, but they are cold for different reasons. The climate in mountains is cold due to high elevation, while the polar regions are cold due to the tilt of the earth. Hear the story of an Ethiopian boy who survives a night in the cold mountains in FIRE ON THE MOUNTAIN *by Jane Kurtz, illustrated by E.B. Lewis, published by Simon & Schuster, 1994. Then, learn about the polar lands with* DRAW•WRITE•NOW®, BOOK FOUR *by Marie Hablitzel and Kim Stitzer, published by Barker Creek Publishing, 1997.*

WHY WOULD A CROCODILE NEED TO HIDE? Page 22

A crocodile hides because it wants to sneak up on other animals and eat them! Follow a hungry crocodile in CROCODILE BEAT *by Gail Jorgensen, illustrated by Patricia Mullins, published by Bradbury, 1989. Then, see how land becomes a mountain peak or a seaside beach with* THE SUN, THE WIND AND THE RAIN *by Lisa Westberg Peters, illustrated by Ted Rand, published by Henry Holt, 1988.*

Ponds & Rivers

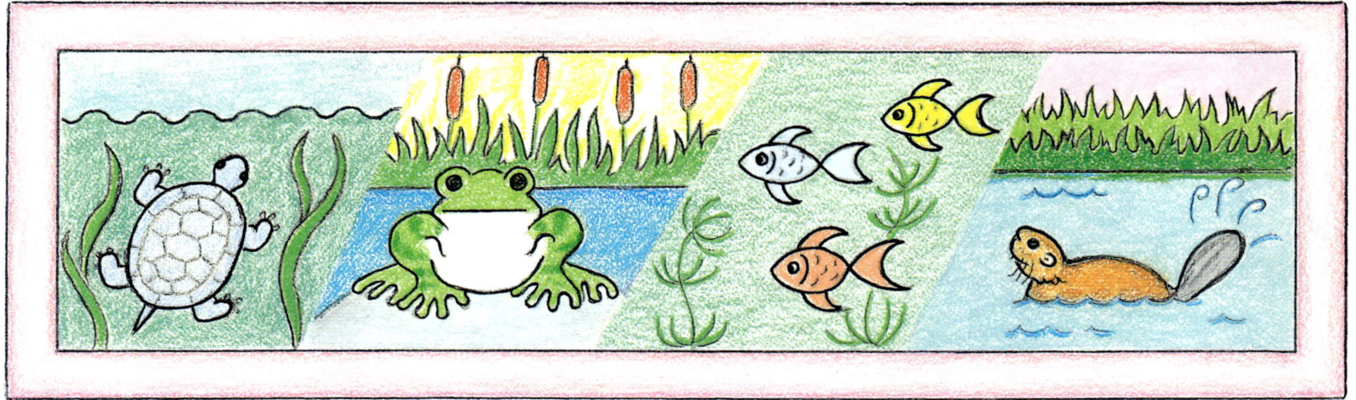

Freshwater Animals

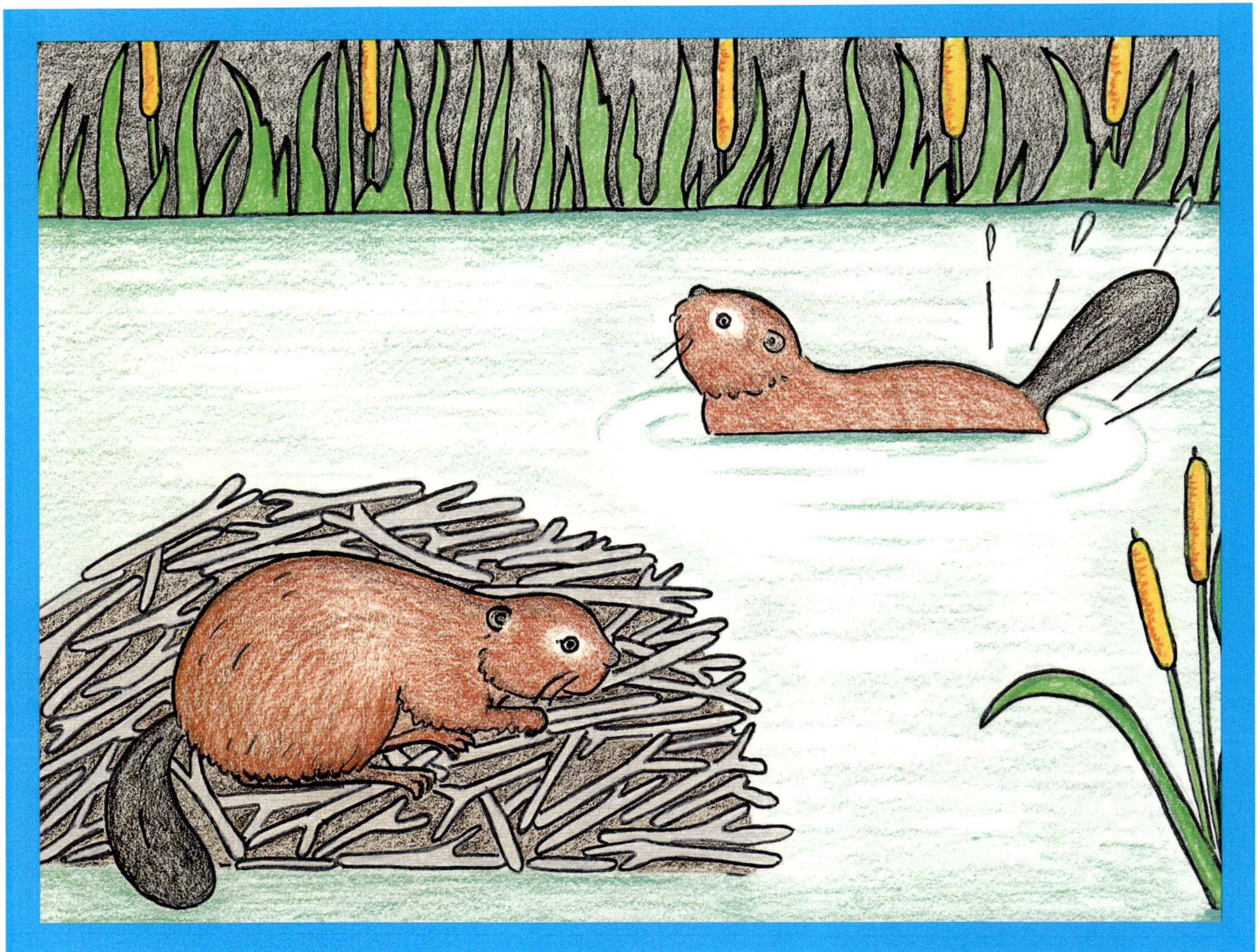

Freshwater homes include shallow still water, deep still water and flowing water.

Water flows and pools on land.
Sometimes water freezes.
Land animals drink water.
Many animals live in it.

Do beavers live in flowing, pooled or frozen water?

Water Homes

Question answered on page 42

Beaver

1.

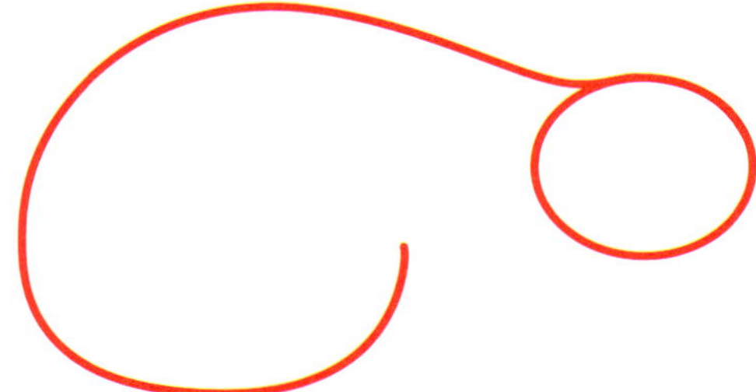

2.

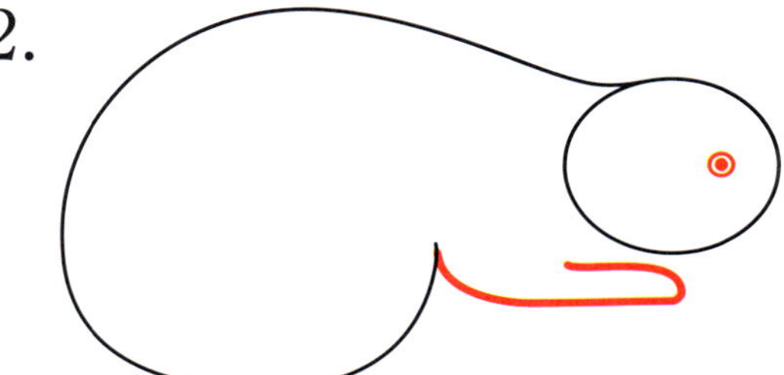

3.

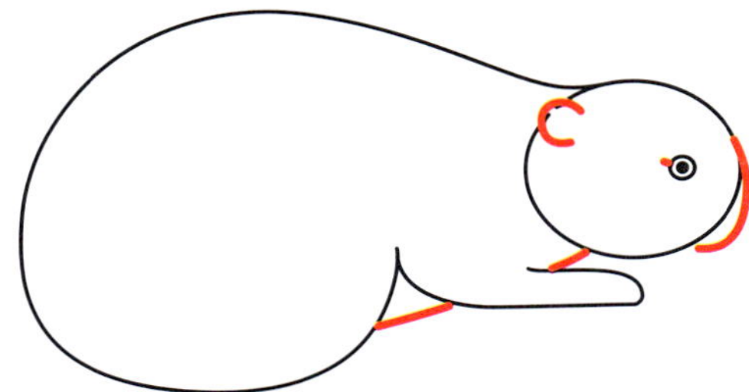

4.

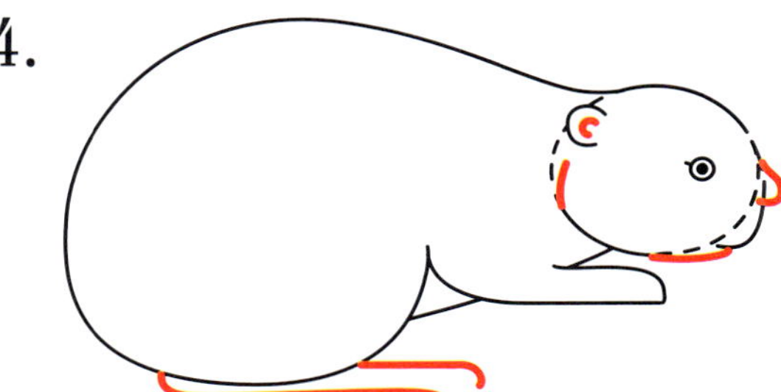

5.

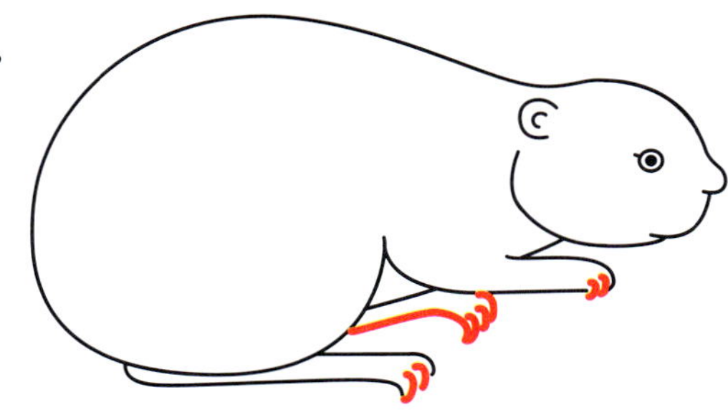

6.

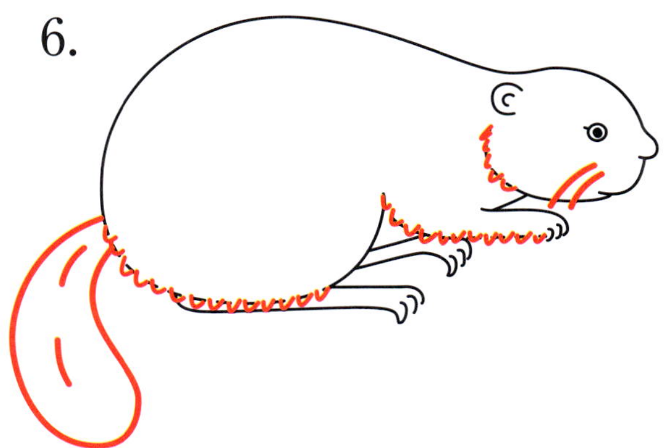

1.

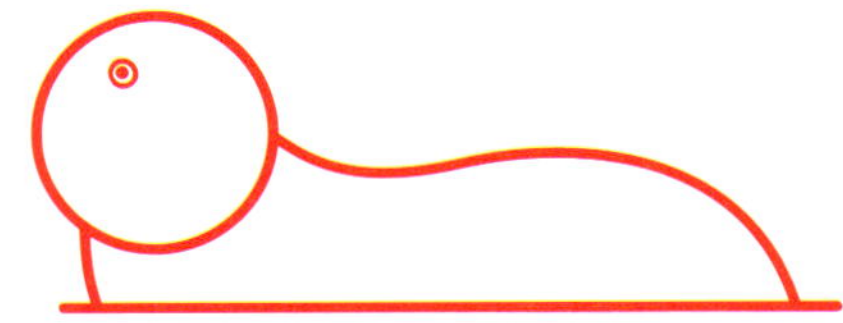

2.

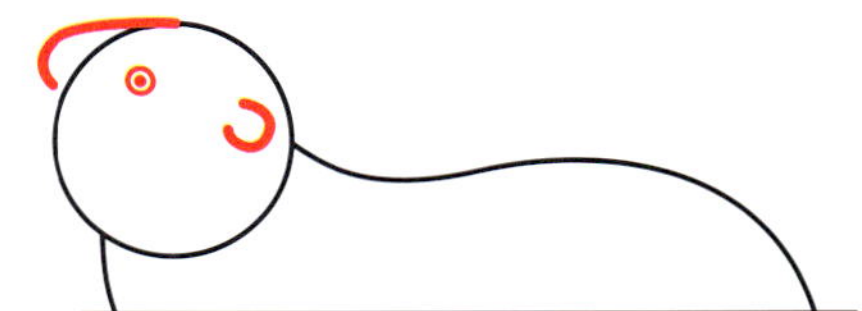

3.

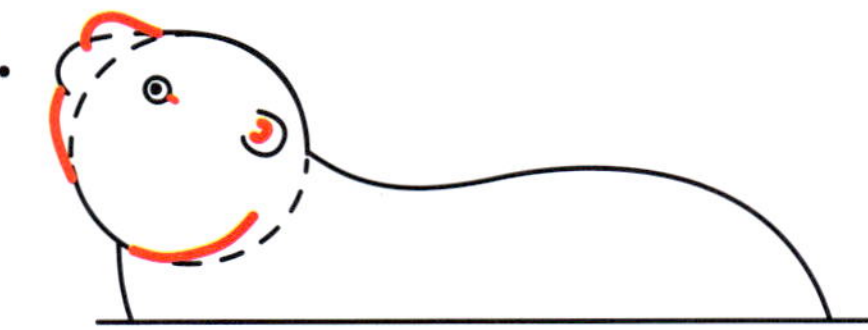

4.

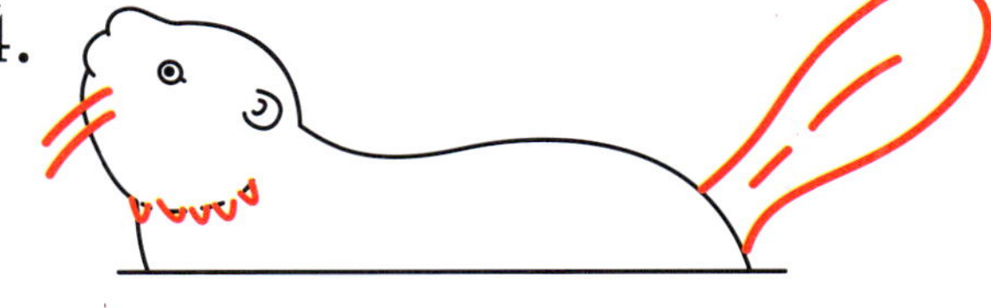

Shallow Water

Teaching Tip on page 64
Question answered on page 42

Frog

1.

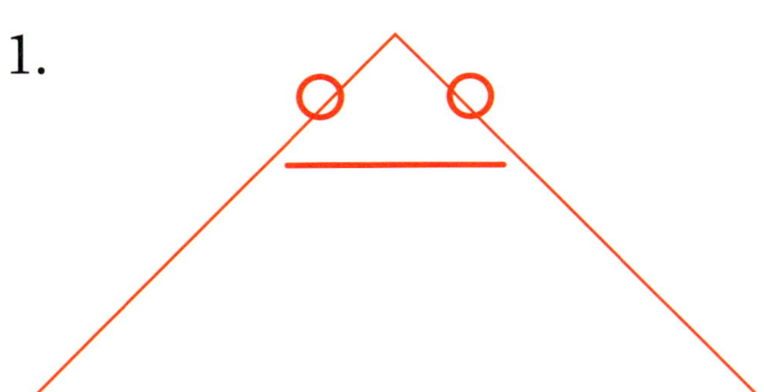

2.

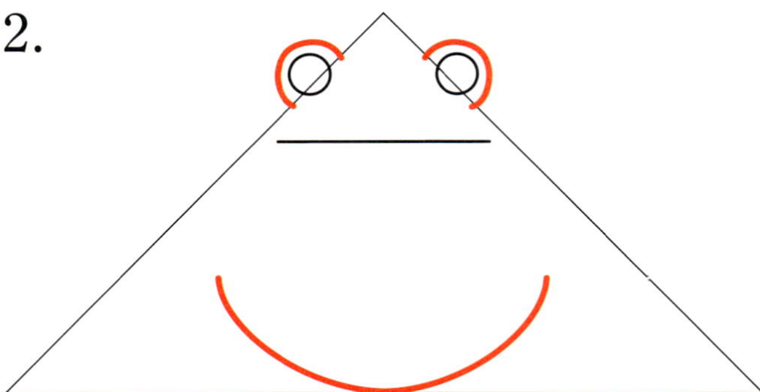

3.

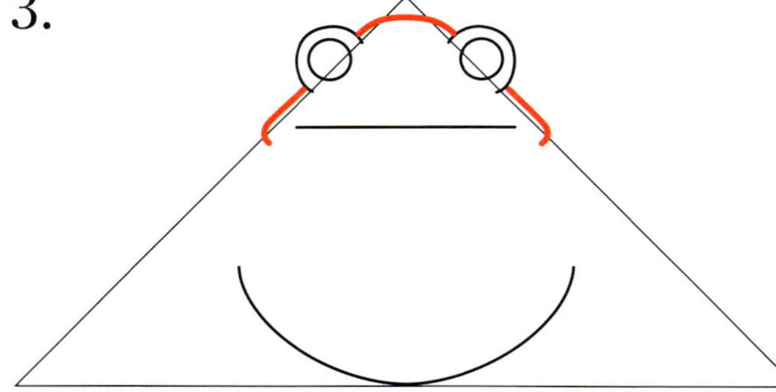

4.

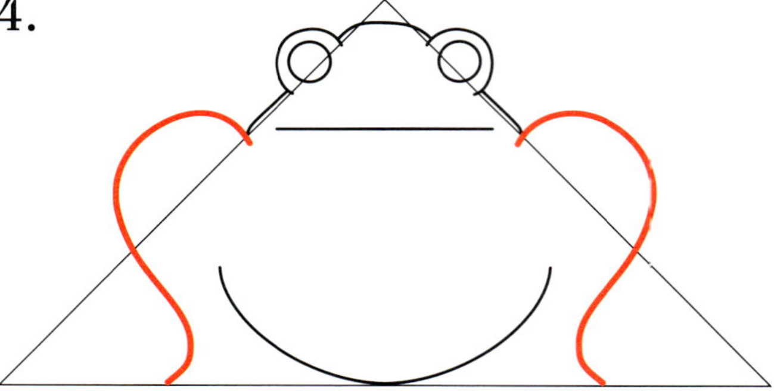

5.

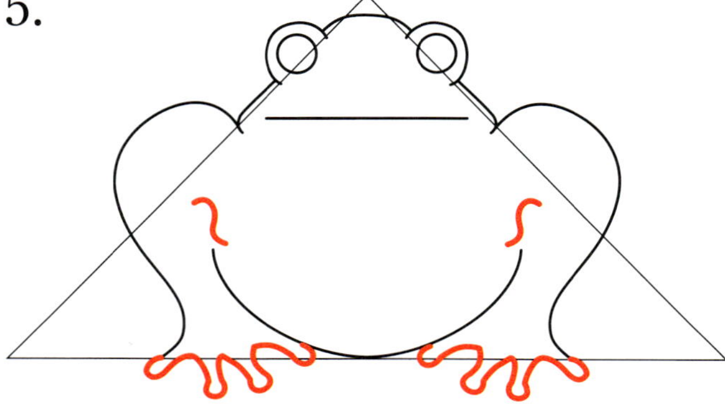

6.

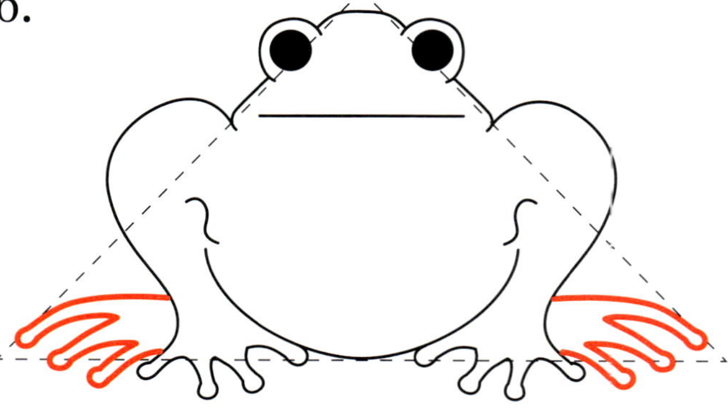

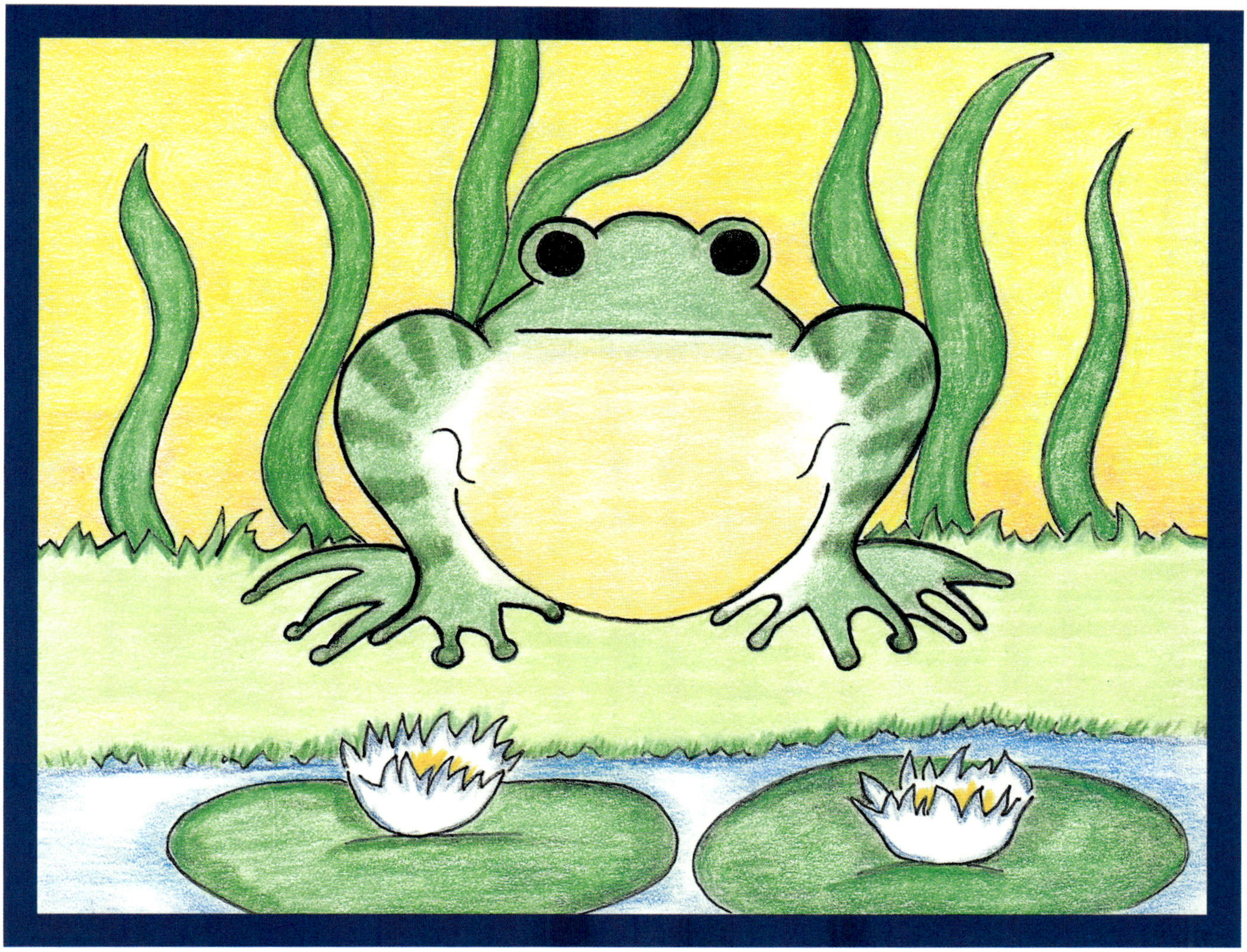

Water is shallow in marshes, swamps, potholes, bogs, fens, vernal ponds, sloughs, ditches and banks.

Water pools on land in wetlands.

The land is muddy and squishy.

The water is shallow and still.

Frogs like still water.

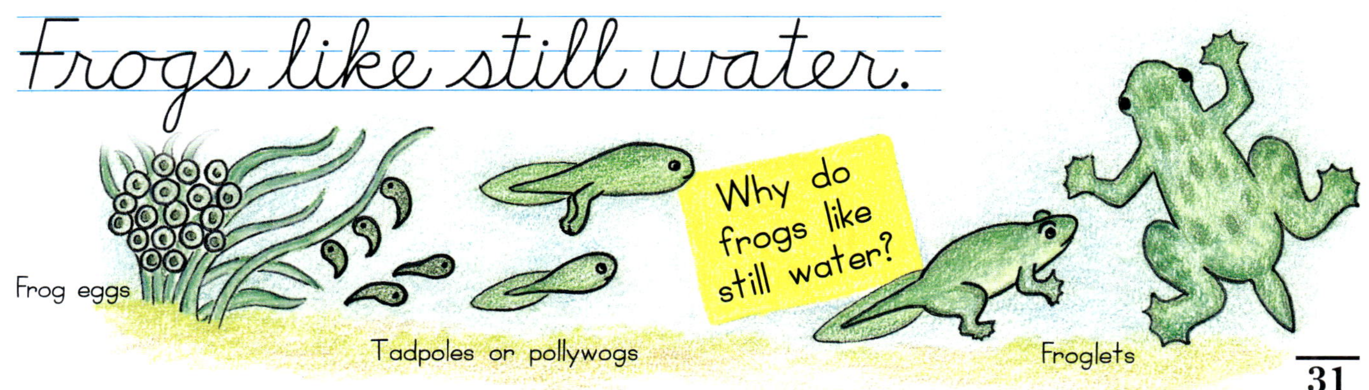

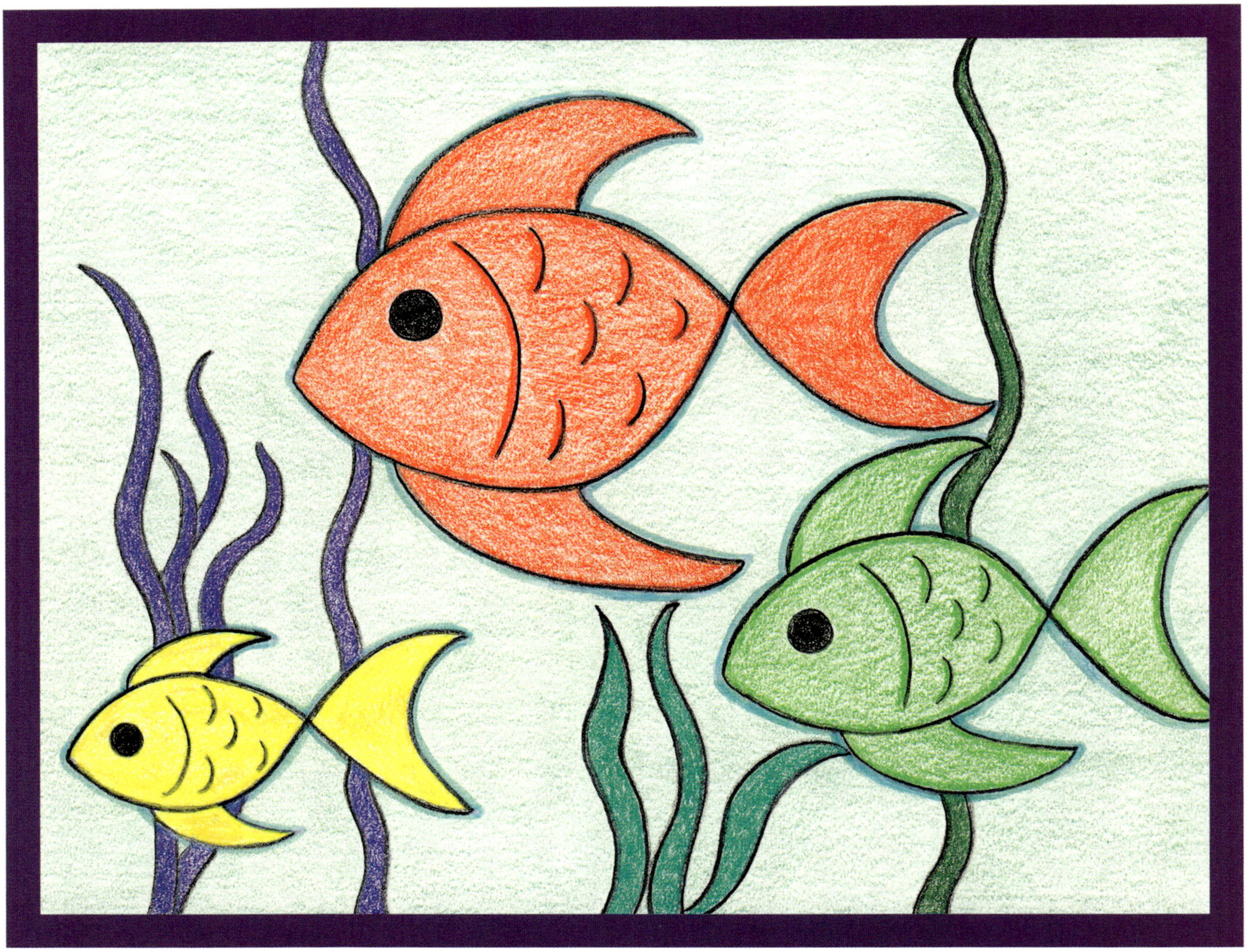

Water is deep in lakes, ponds and reservoirs.

Land has deep pools of water.
These are lakes and ponds.
Some animals stay in water.
They get oxygen from water.

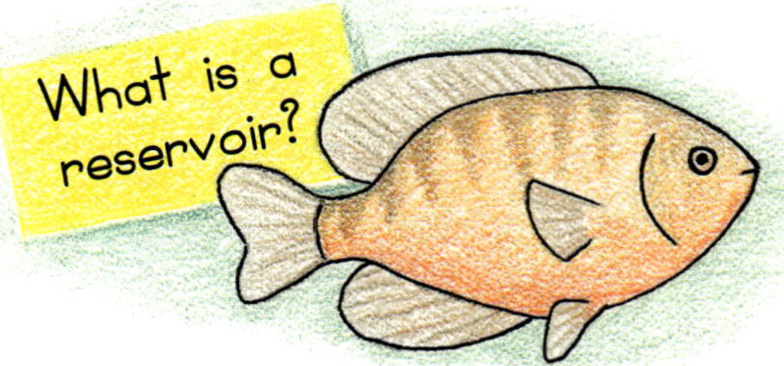

Deep Water

Teaching Tip on page 64
Question answered on page 42

Fish

1.

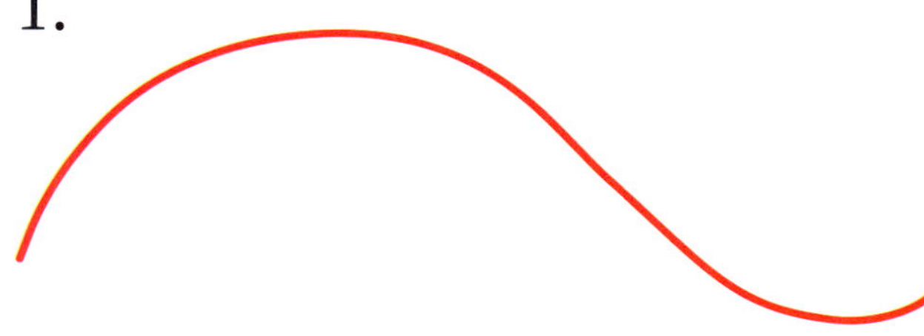

2.

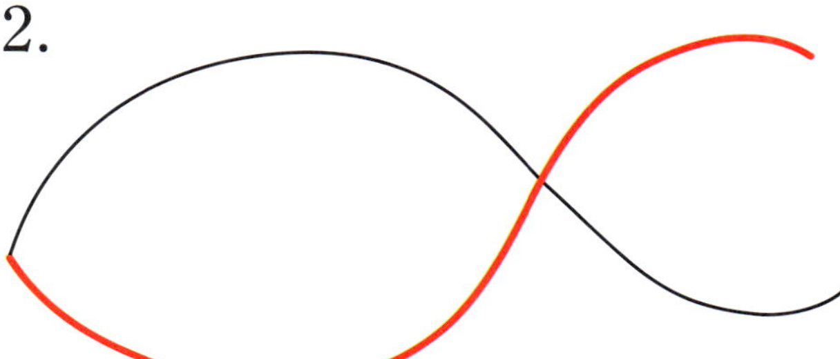

3.

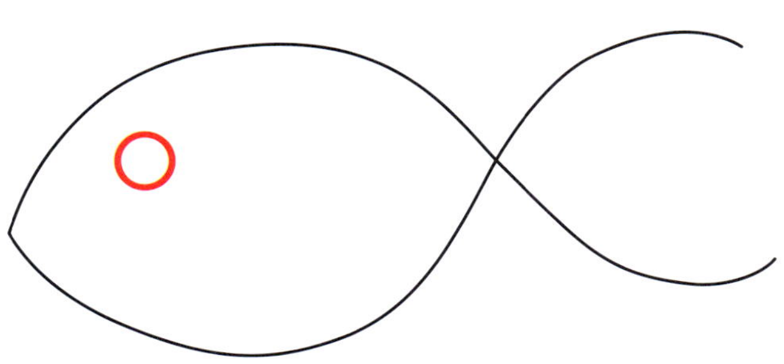

4.

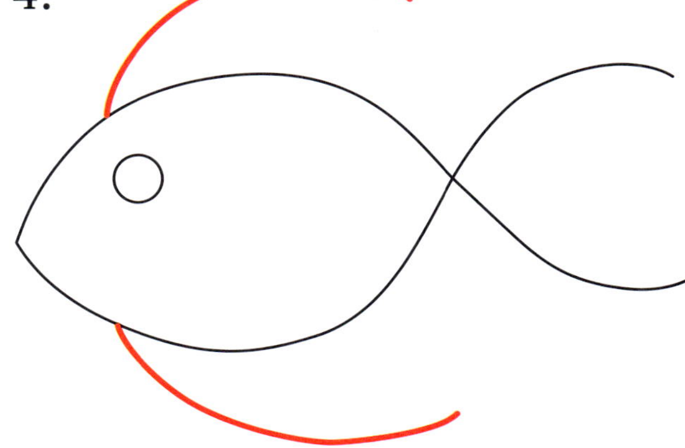

5.

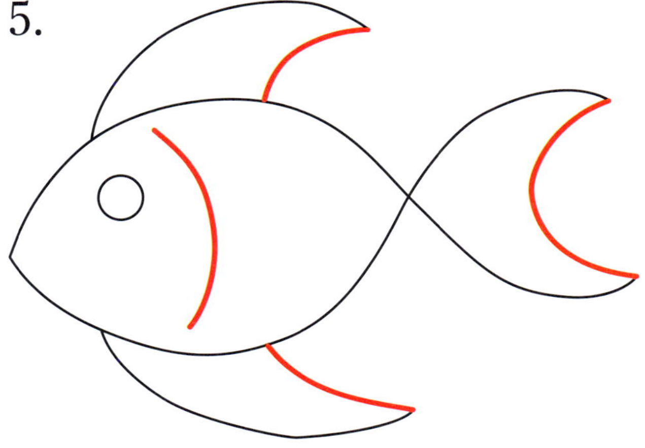

6.

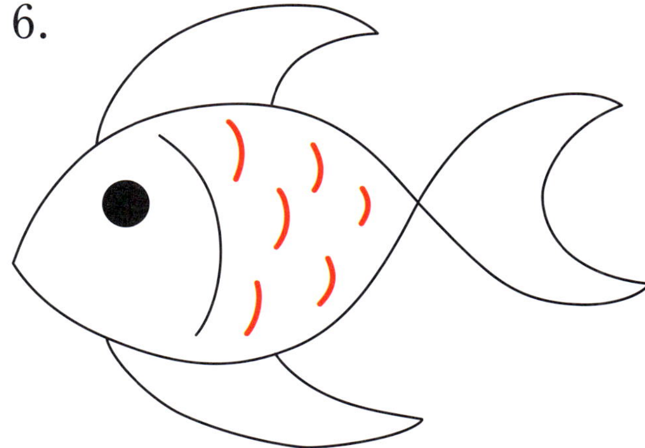

Flowing Water

Question answered on page 42

Turtle

1.

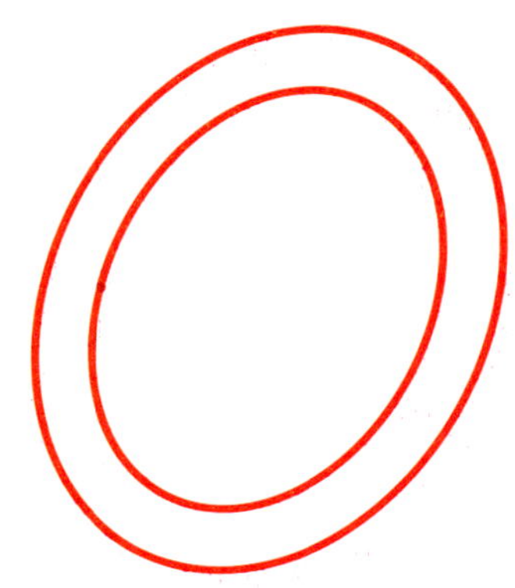

2.

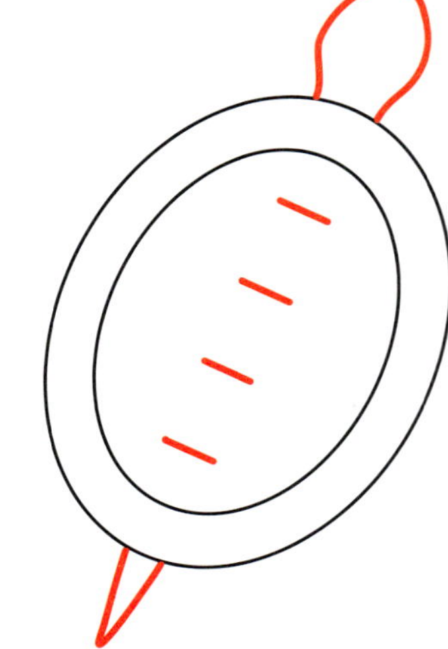

3.

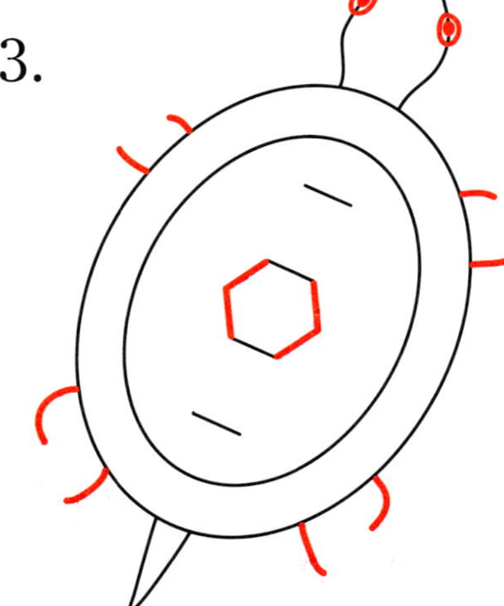

4.

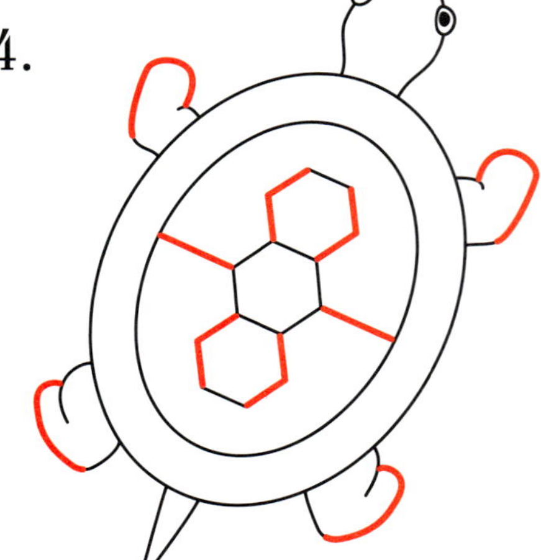

5.

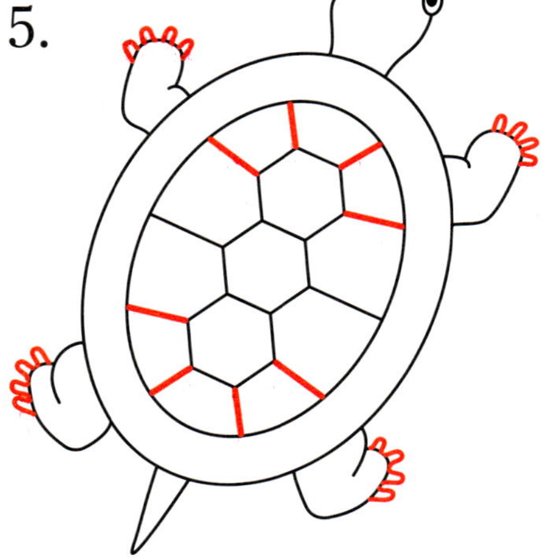

6.

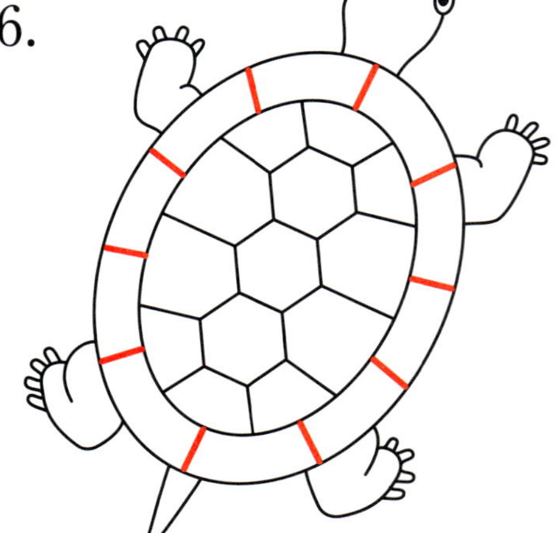

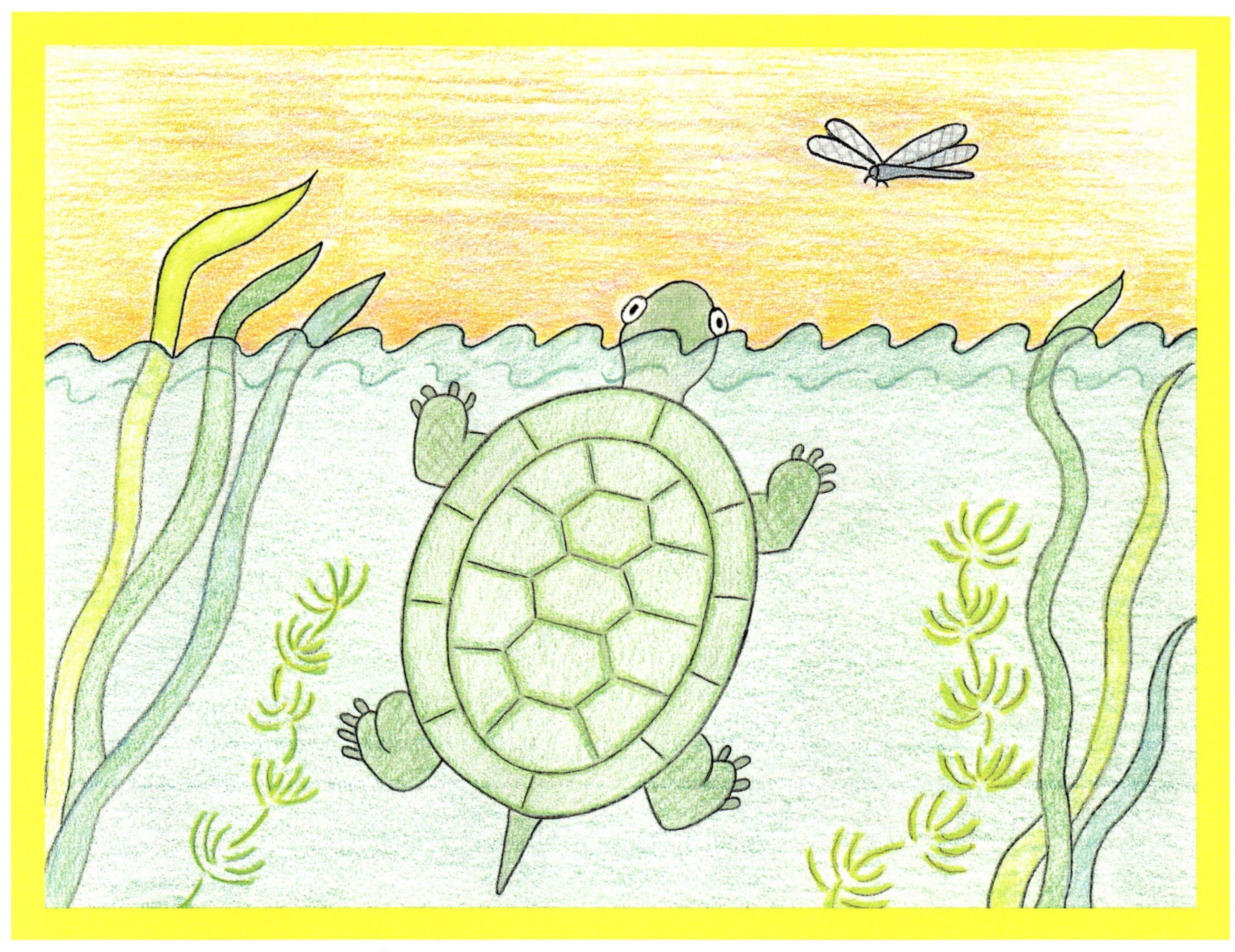

Water flows in rivers, streams, creeks, brooks and rivulets.

Water on land flows downhill.
It flows in streams or rivers.
Water rushes over steep land.
It moves slowly on flat land.

Where do turtles sleep?

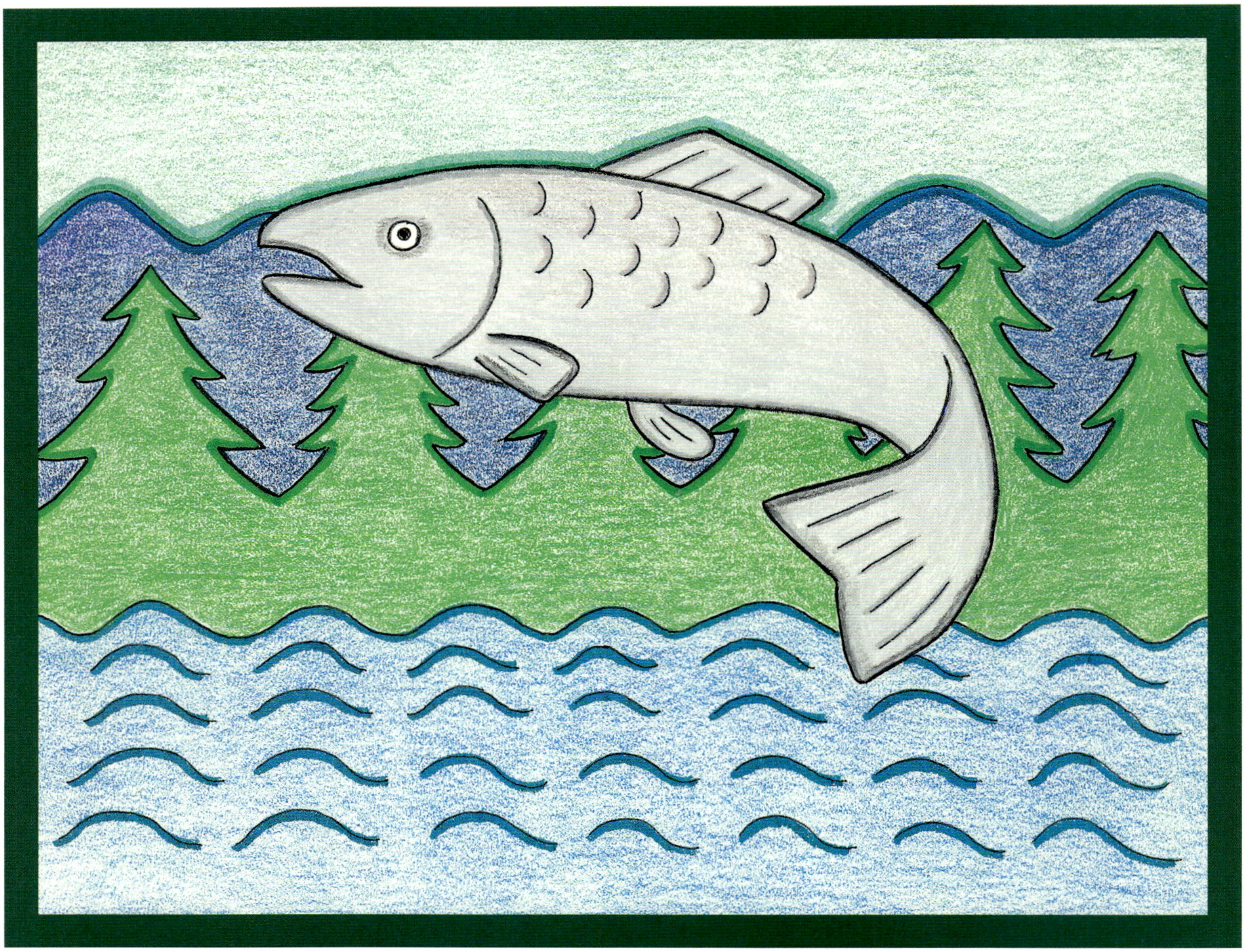

Salmon migrate from freshwater to saltwater and back to freshwater.

Some streams flow into rivers.
Most rivers flow to oceans.
Salmon eggs hatch in streams.
Young salmon swim to the ocean.

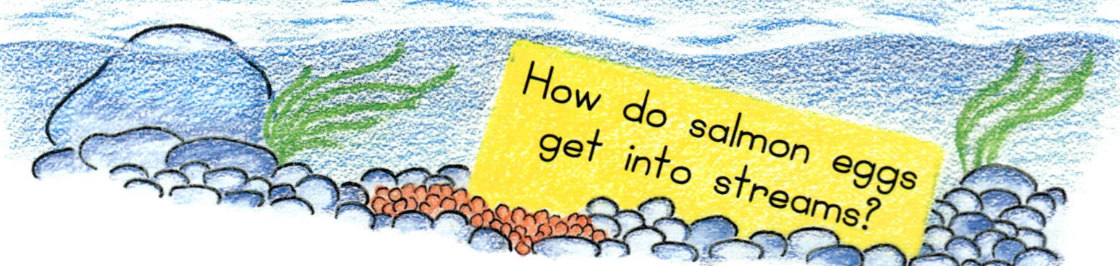

Stream to River to Ocean

Question answered on page 42

Salmon

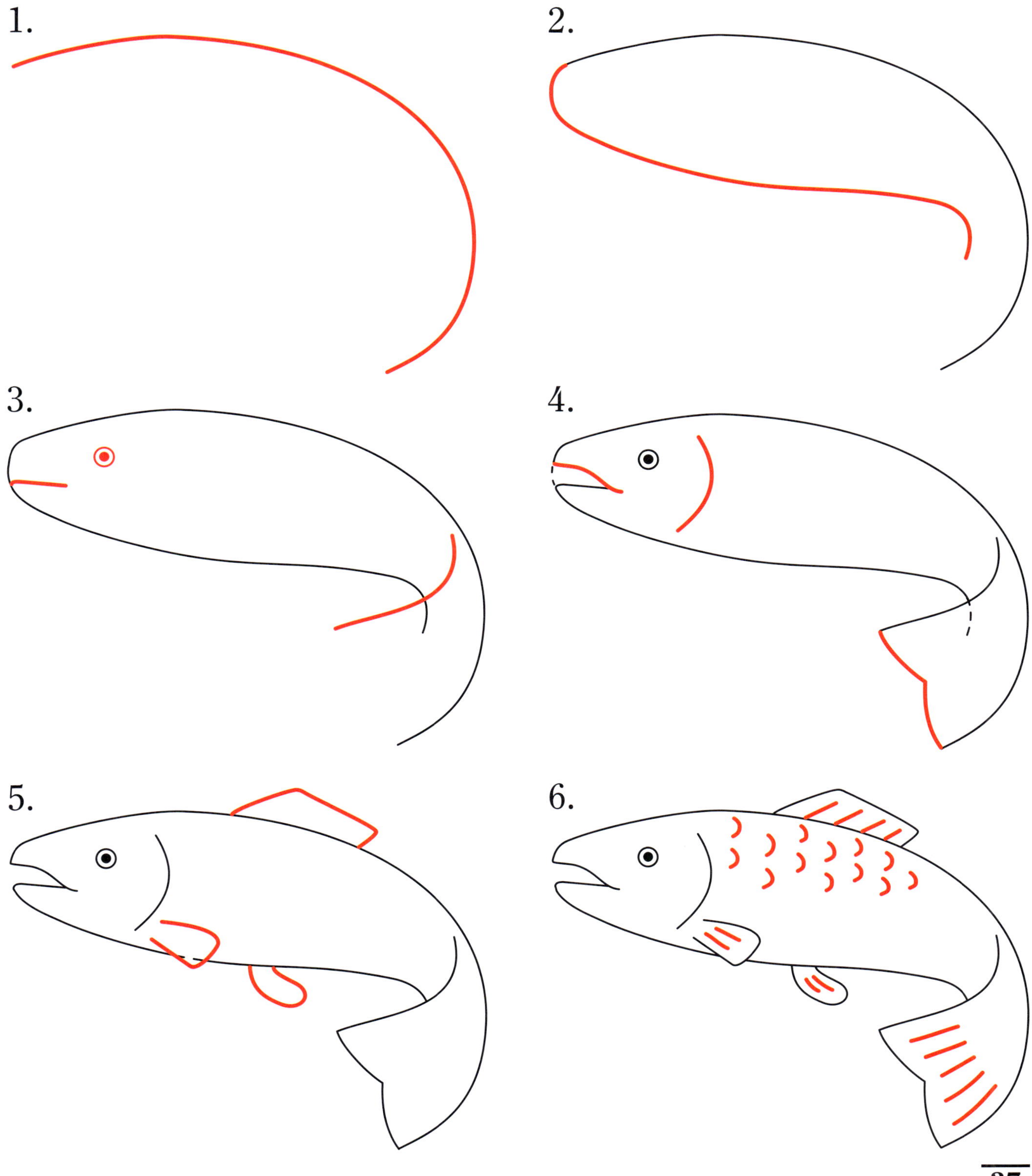

Ocean to River to Stream

Teaching Tip on page 64
Question answered on page 42

Eel

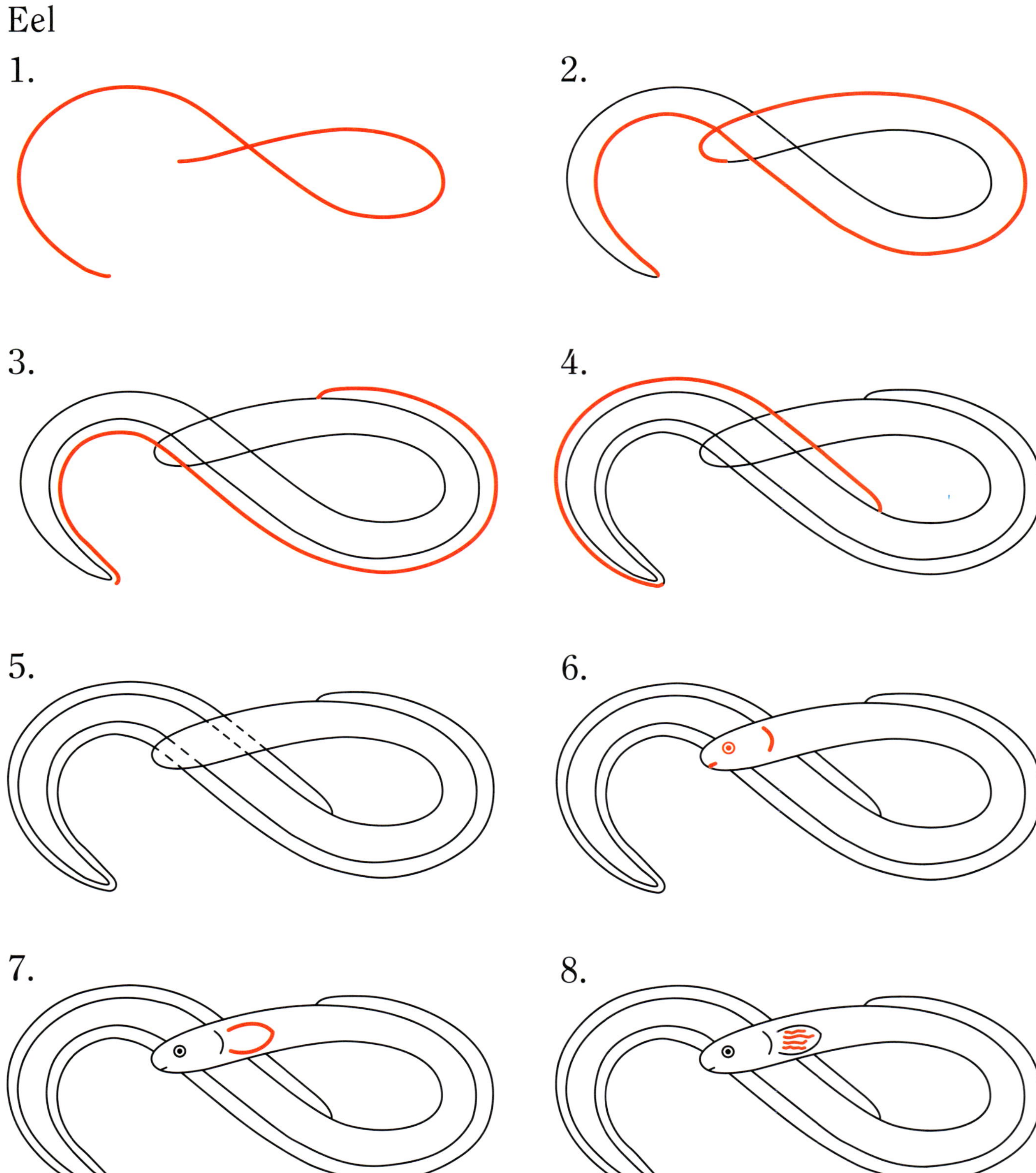

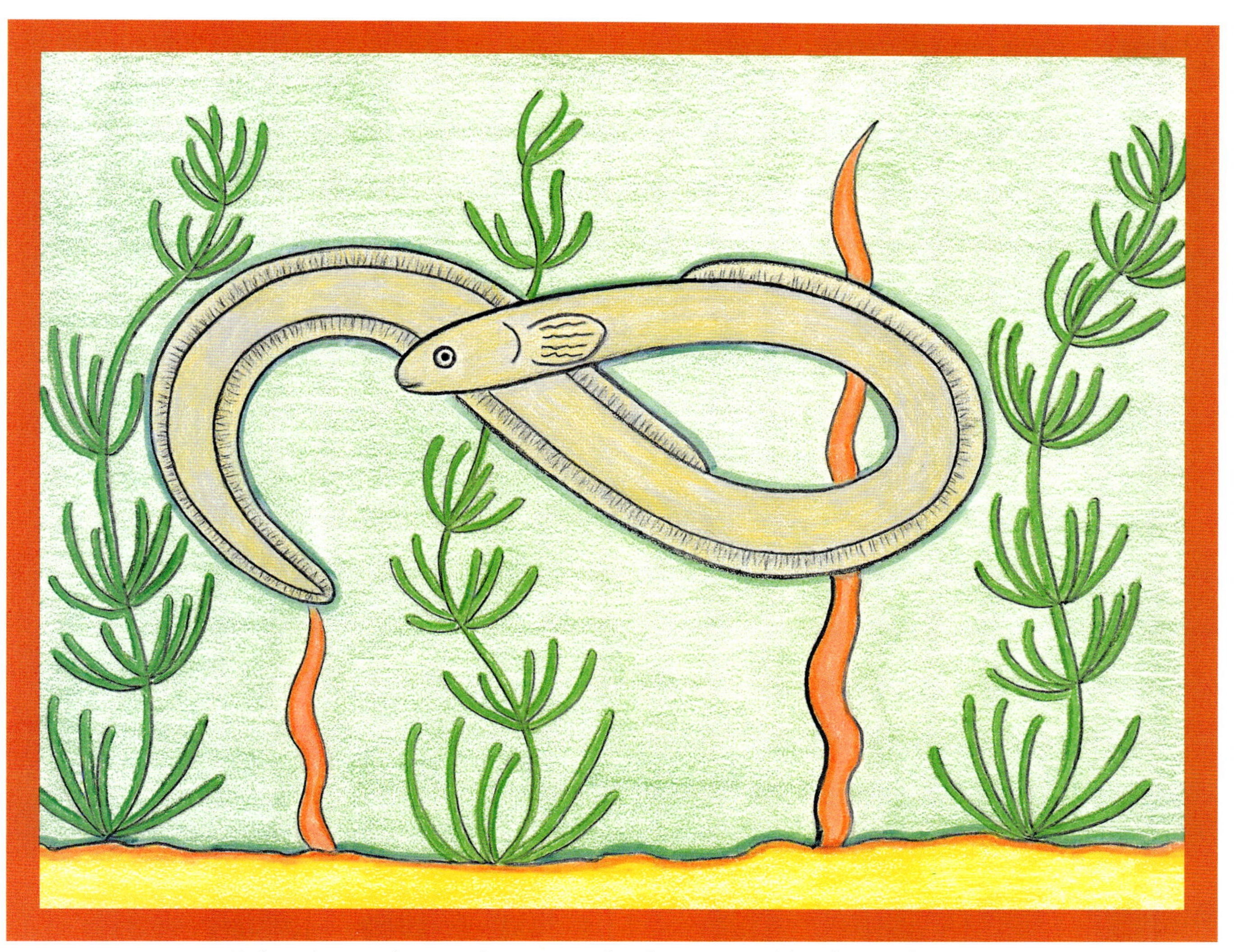

Eels migrate from saltwater to freshwater and back to saltwater.

Eel eggs hatch in the ocean.
Young eels swim to rivers.
They swim upstream and grow.
They return to the sea.

Why do young eels travel to rivers and streams?

Draw Your World

Look through a window. Where is the horizon line? Does the horizon line move when you move up or down?

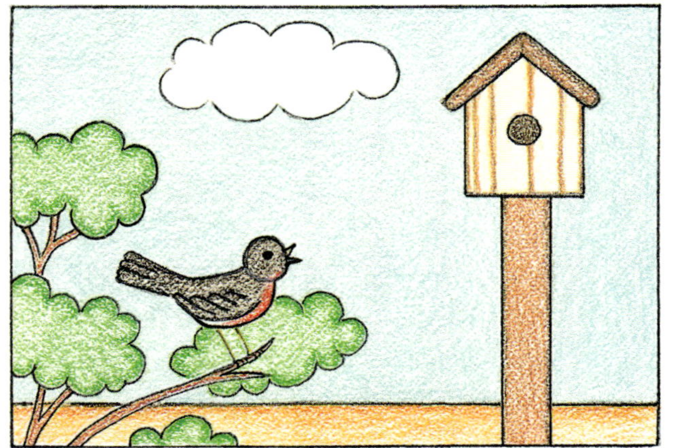

Is the horizon line near the bottom of the window?

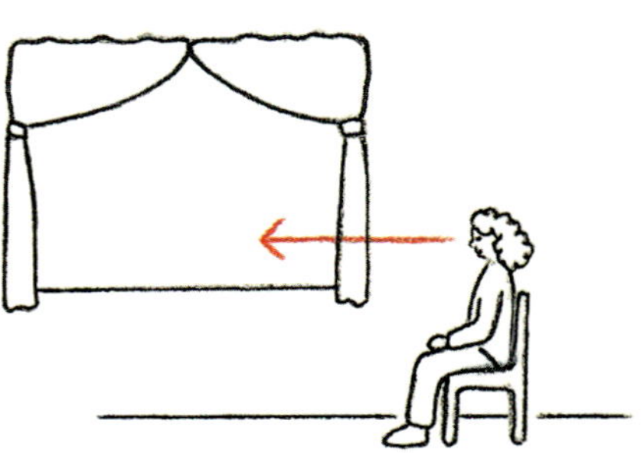

Is the horizon line in the middle of the window?

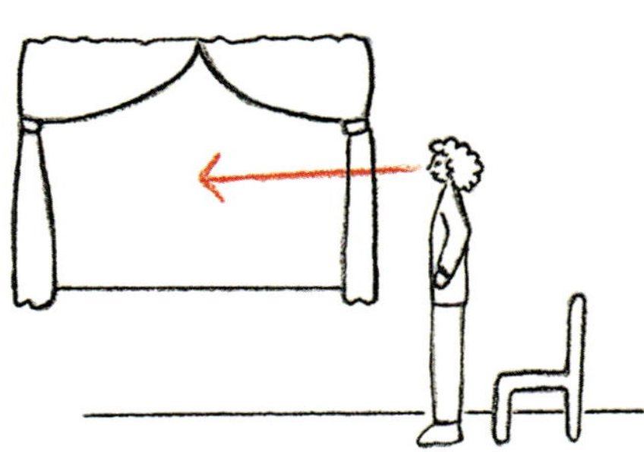

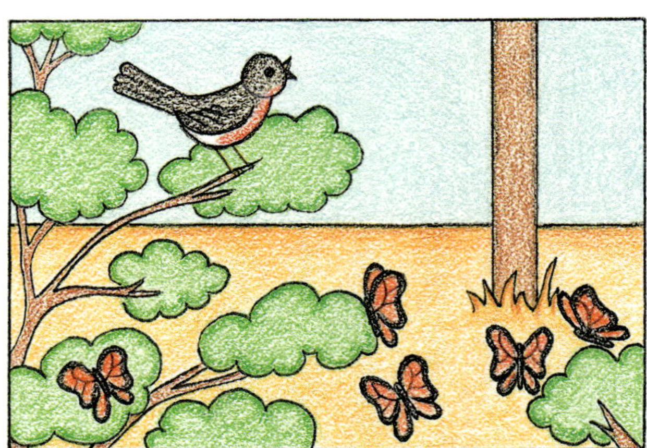

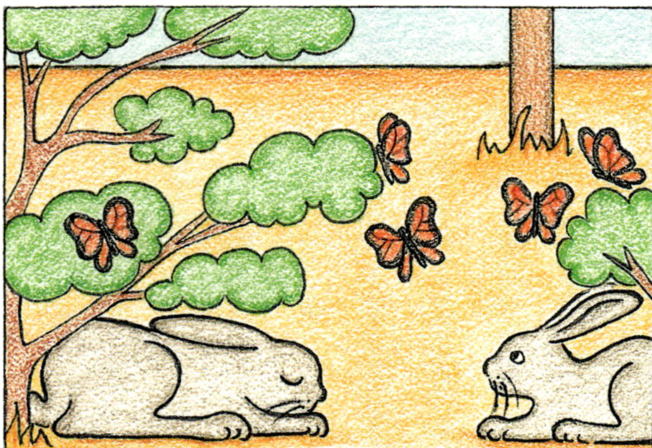

Is the horizon line near the top of the window?

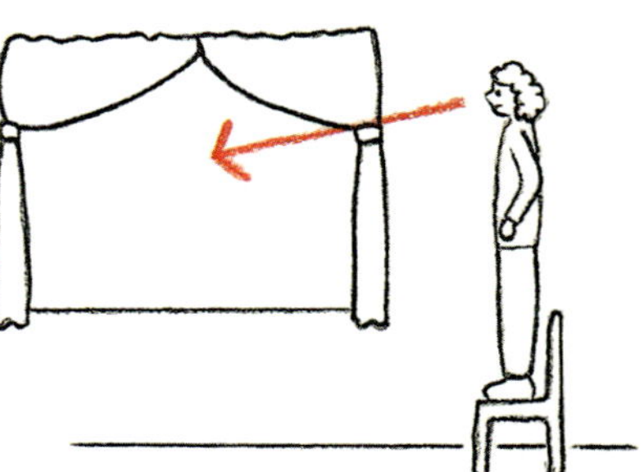

Pretend the edges of the window are the edges of a piece of drawing paper.

Start your background with a line . . .

Draw a line to show where the sky meets the earth.

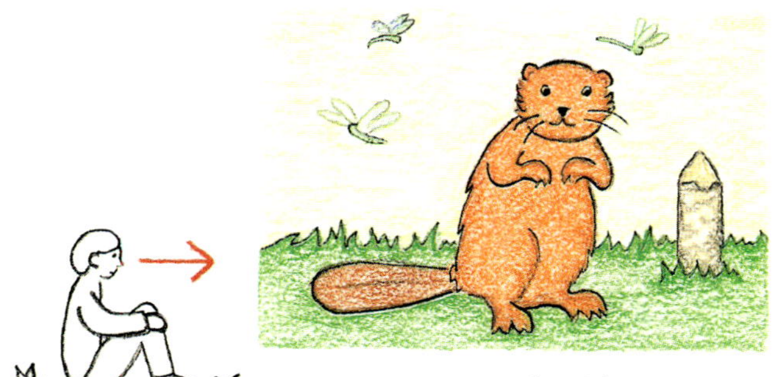

Mostly Sky
(pages 10, 13, 17, 21 and 31)

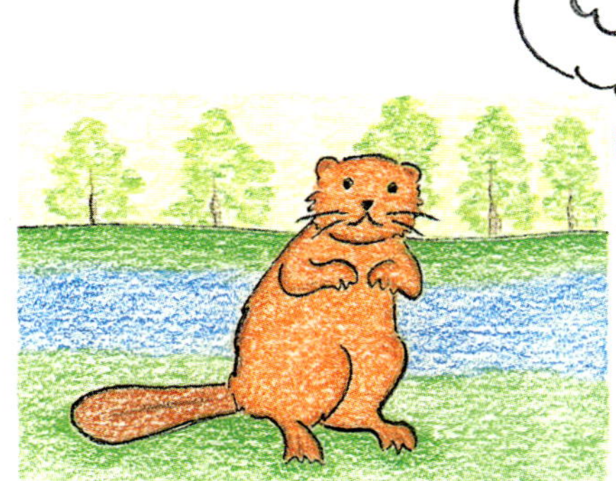

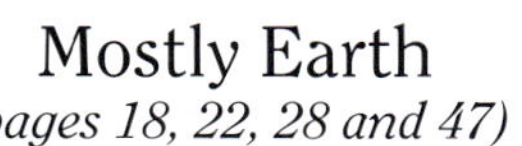

Mostly Earth
(pages 18, 22, 28 and 47)

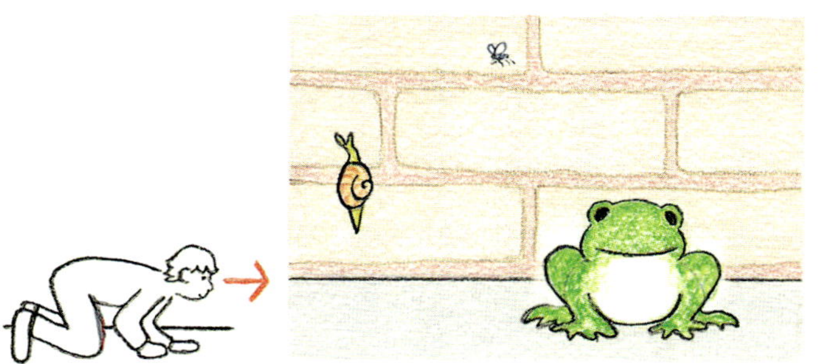

Mostly Wall

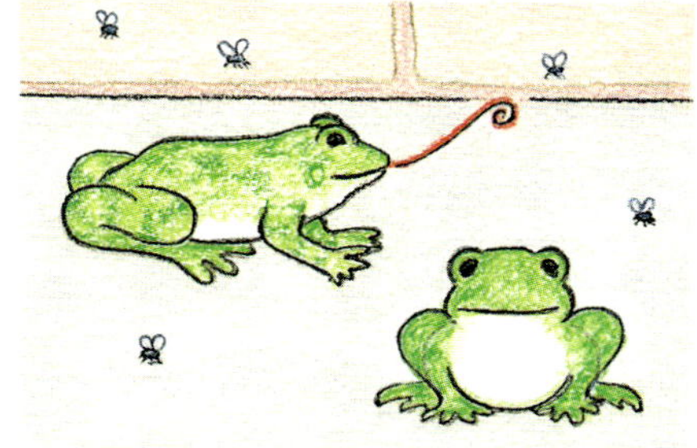

Mostly Floor

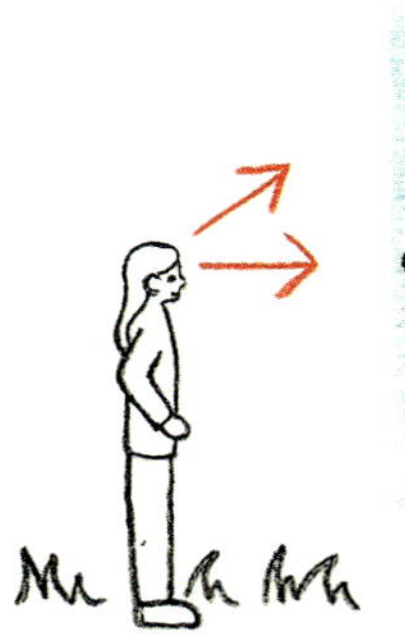

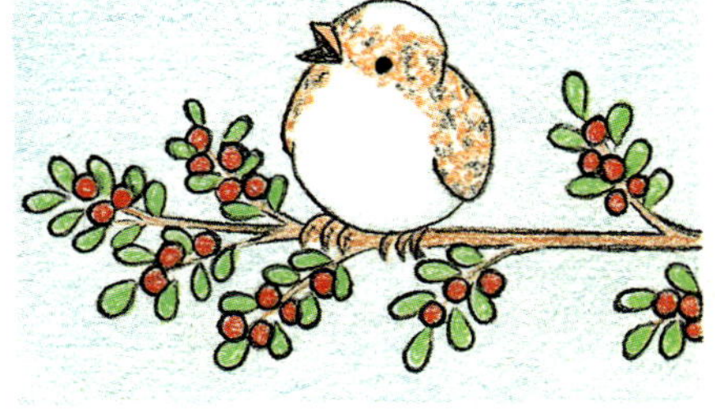

All Sky
(page 14)

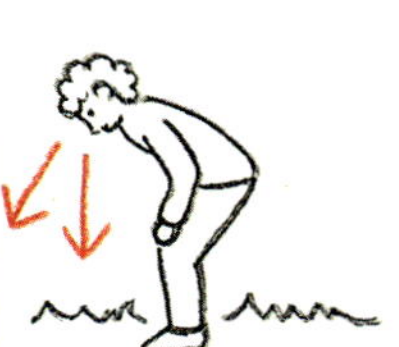

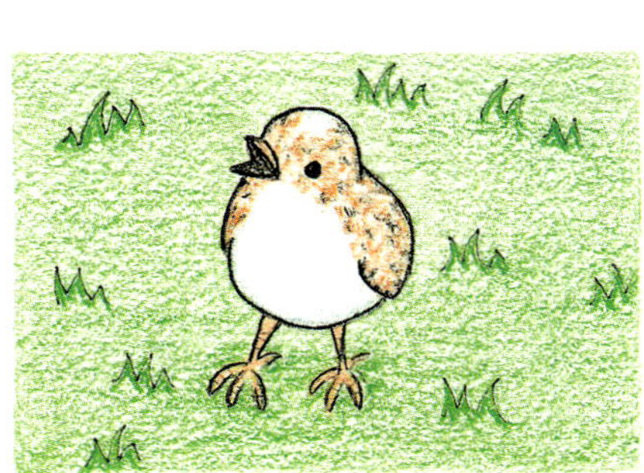

All Earth
(page 48)

Learn more about ponds and rivers...

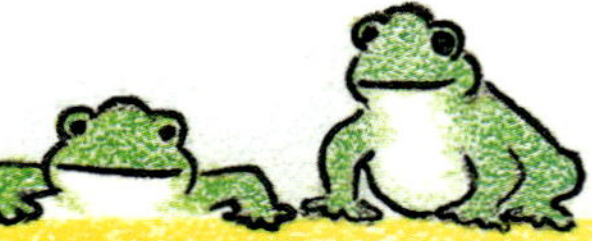

DO BEAVERS LIVE IN FLOWING, POOLED OR FROZEN WATER? Page 28

They live in all three. Beavers find a stream (flowing water), slow the flow by building a dam to create a pond (pooled water), then rest safely during winter beneath snow and ice (frozen water). Watch the busy beavers who build a dam and lodge in THINK OF A BEAVER *by Karen Wallace, illustrated by Mick Manning, published by Candlewick Press, 1993.*

Water is always moving on our planet. See the various paths water takes with FOLLOW THE WATER FROM BROOK TO OCEAN *written and illustrated by Arthur Dorros, published by HarperCollins, 1991. Then, follow water as a vapor, liquid and solid from a rocky coast in Maine to a rooftop in Spain to a peak in the Alps and beyond in* A DROP AROUND THE WORLD *by Barbara Shaw McKinney, illustrated by Michael S. Maydak, published by Dawn, 1998.*

WHY DO FROGS LIKE STILL WATER? Page 31

Frogs, like all amphibians, lay eggs in water. Shallow, still water provides a safe environment for newly hatched pollywogs. Become as small as a frog to understand their need for still, calm water with THE MAGIC SCHOOL BUS HOPS HOME *by Patricia Relf, illustrated by Nancy Stevenson, published by Scholastic, 1995.*

Learn the importance of wet, soggy places with SQUISH! A WETLAND WALK *by Nancy Luenn, illustrated by Ronald Himler, published by Macmillan, 1994. Then, see how life in and around a vernal lake changes as the water within it diminishes in* DISAPPEARING LAKE *by Debbie S. Miller, illustrated by Jon Van Zyle, published by Walker, 1997.*

WHAT IS A RESERVOIR? Page 32

People dam rivers and streams, much like beavers dam streams. The resulting man-made lake or pond is called a reservoir. To create a new environment, another environment is usually destroyed. Watch how a small farmland town is destroyed so a reservoir may be created in LETTING SWIFT RIVER GO *by Jane Yolen, illustrated by Barbara Cooney, published by Little, Brown & Co., 1992.*

WHERE DO TURTLES SLEEP? Page 35

Turtles sleep in their shells. Because they carry their homes on their backs, turtles have shelter wherever they go. See THE TURTLE AND THE MOON *by Charles Turner, illustrated by Melissa Bay Mathis, published by Dutton, 1991. The reflection of the moon on the water's surface becomes a young turtle's playmate.*

Most people think of the Mississippi River as a big, mighty river, but its headwaters flow slowly and are dotted with lily pads. Travel the headwaters by canoe with MISSISSIPPI GOING NORTH *by Sanna Anderson Baker, illustrated by Bill Farnsworth, published by Albert Whitman, 1996. Compare the Mississippi's headwaters to the swiftly flowing water of a mountain stream in* THE PERFECT SPOT *written and illustrated by Robert J. Blake, published by Philamel, 1992.*

HOW DO SALMON EGGS GET INTO STREAMS? Page 36

A mature salmon feeds and grows in the ocean for several years. When the time comes to lay eggs, the salmon returns to its stream. Follow the remarkable migration of these strong fish in SWIMMER *by Shelly Gill, illustrated by Shannon Cartwright, published by Paws IV, 1995.*

WHY DO YOUNG EELS TRAVEL TO RIVERS AND STREAMS? Page 39

Like the salmon, eels are migratory. Follow the eels' life cycle with THINK OF AN EEL *by Karen Wallace, illustrated by Mike Bostock, published by Candlewick Press, 1993.*

Oceans

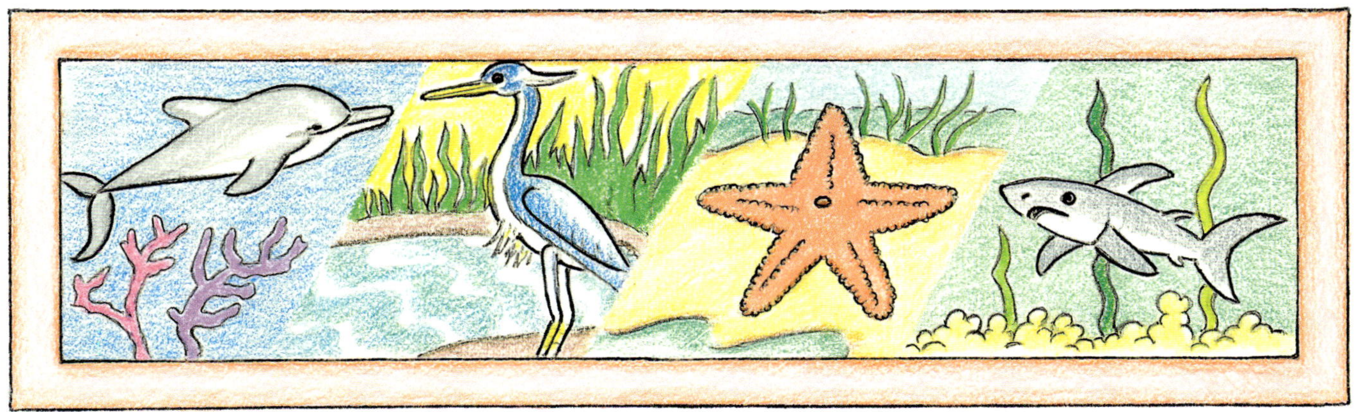

Saltwater Animals

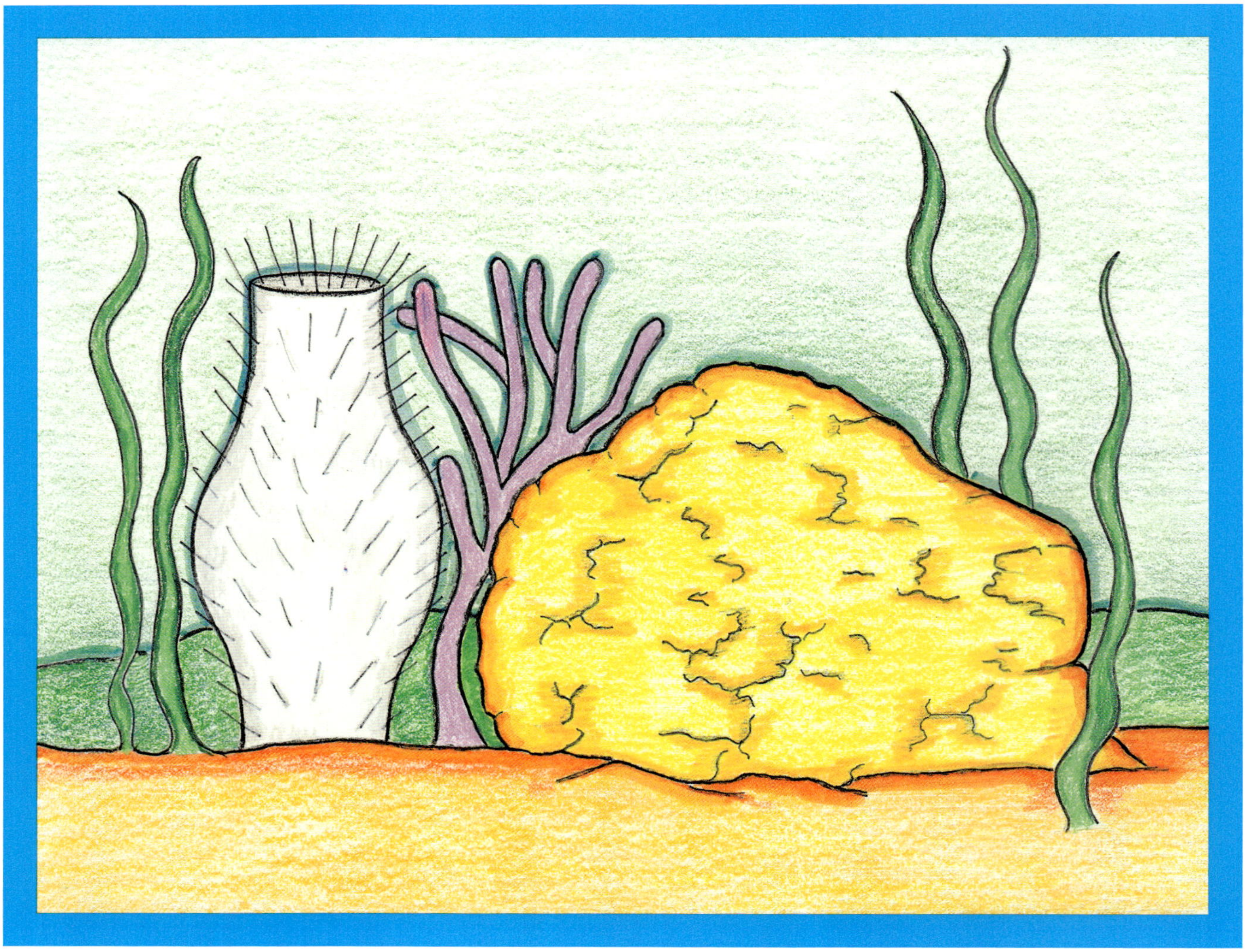

Saltwater homes include tidelands, continental shelves and the open ocean.

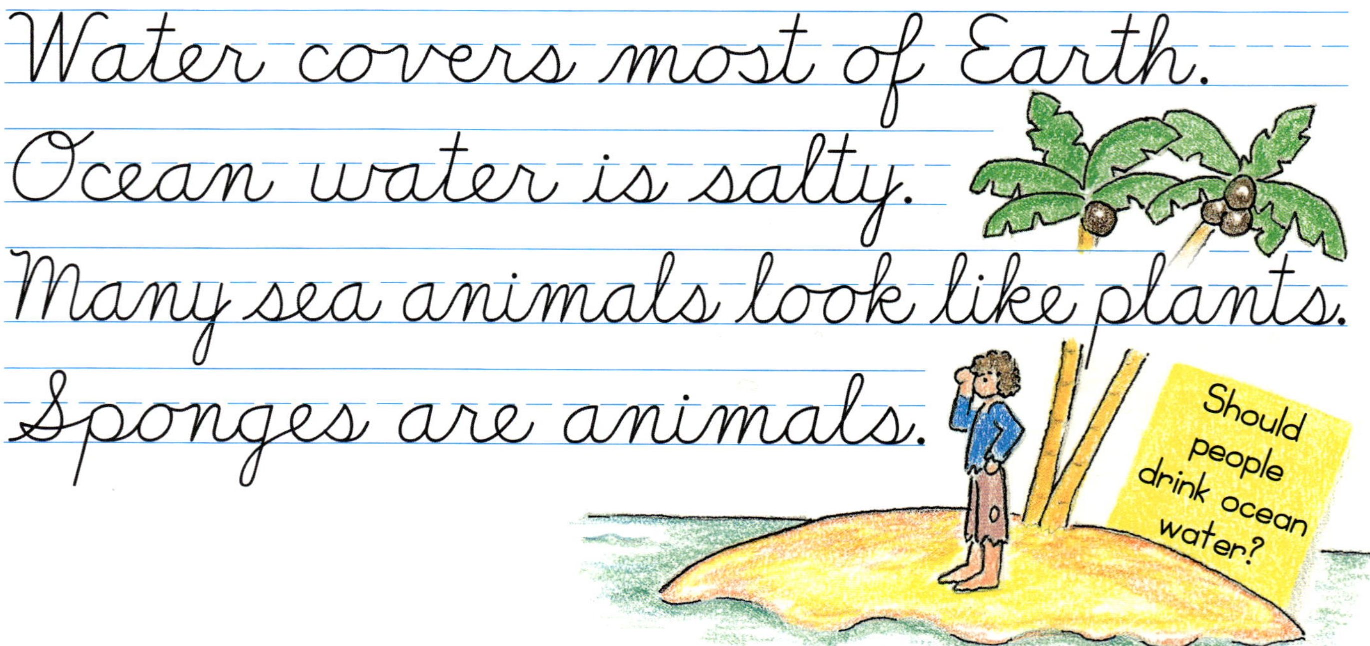

Water covers most of Earth.

Ocean water is salty.

Many sea animals look like plants.

Sponges are animals.

Ocean Homes

Question answered on page 62

Lampshade Sponge

1.

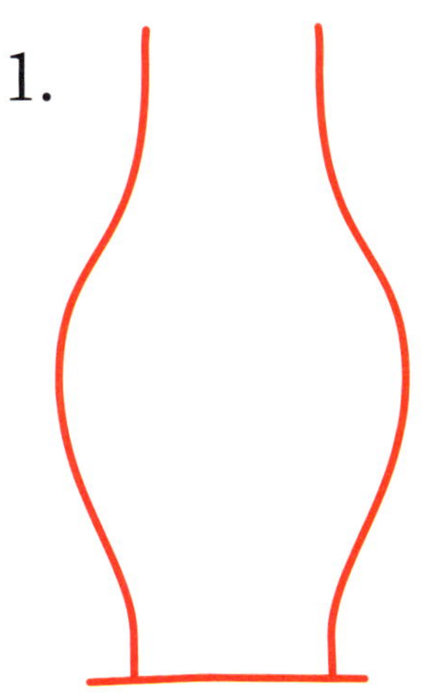

2.

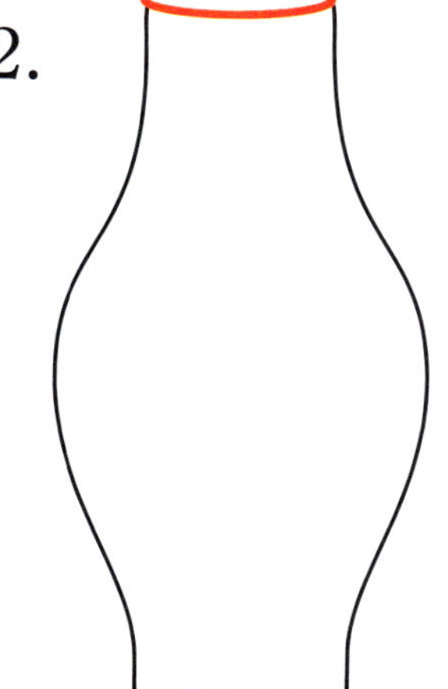

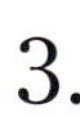

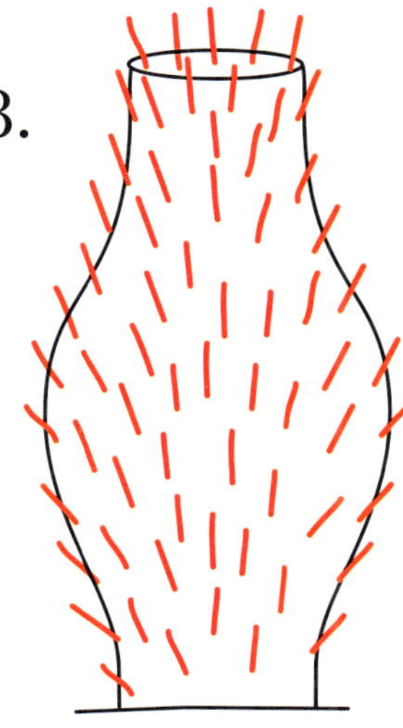

Common Sponge

1.

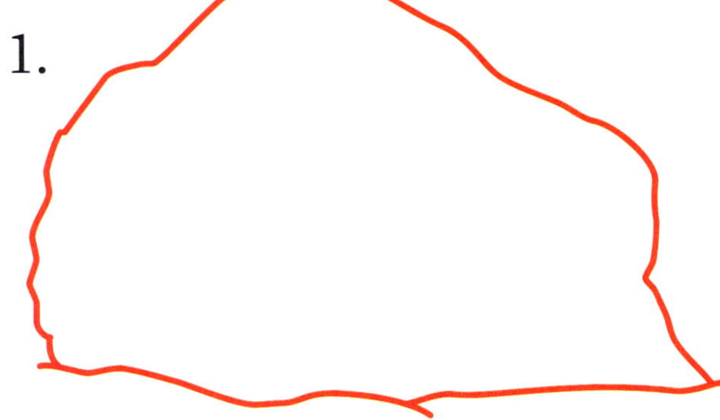

2.

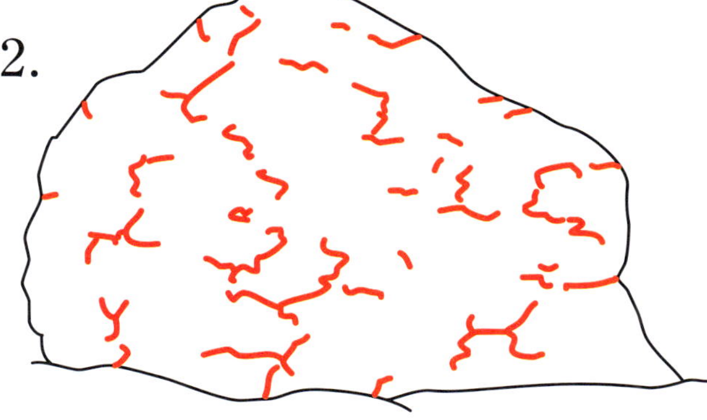

Deadman's Finger Sponge

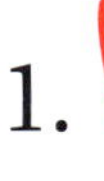

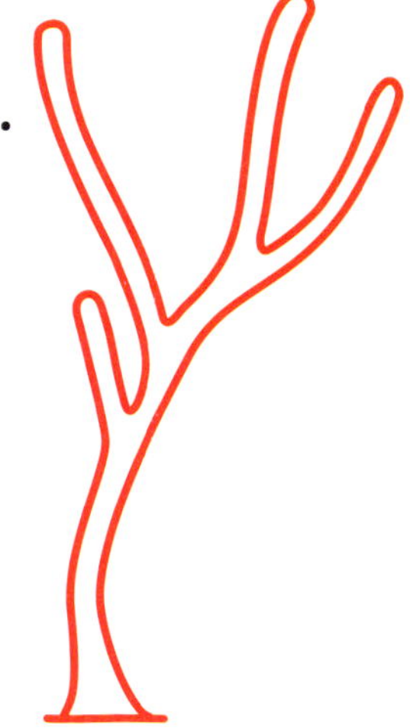

2.

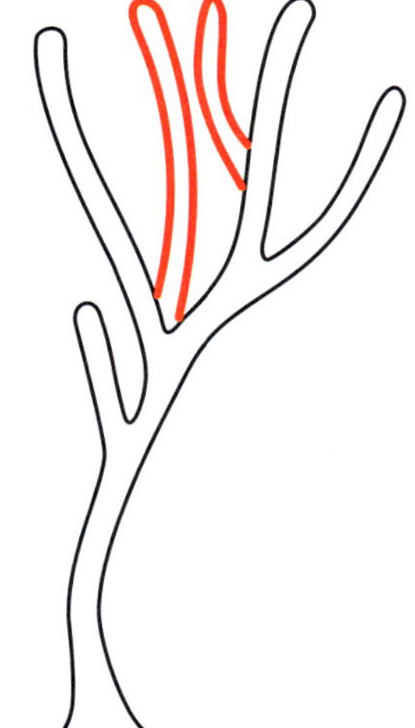

3.

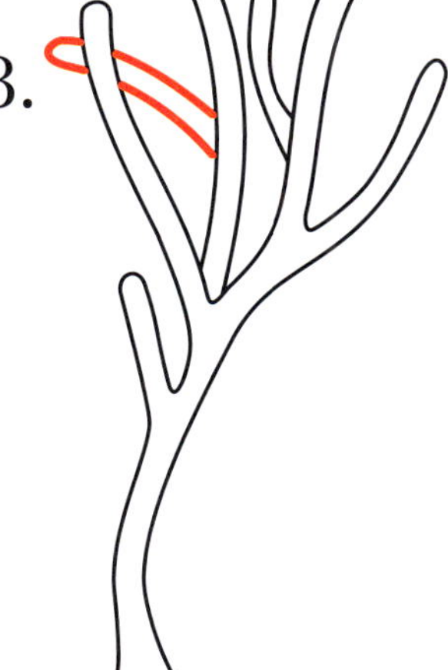

Muddy Tidelands

Question answered on page 62
Teaching Tip on page 64

Great Blue Heron

1.

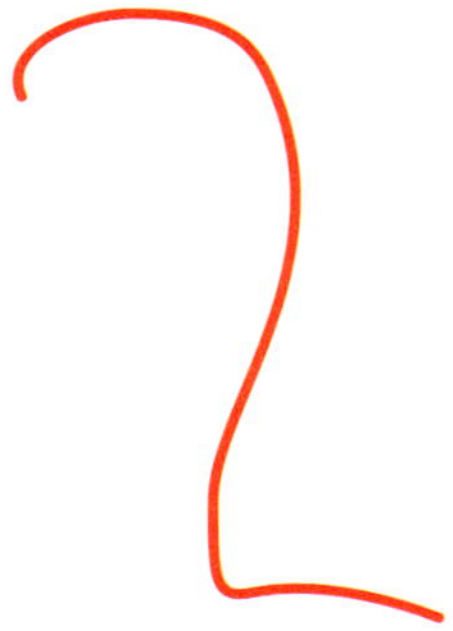

2.

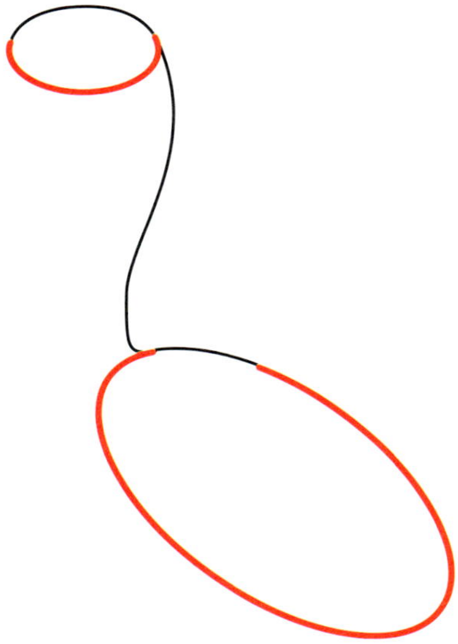

3.

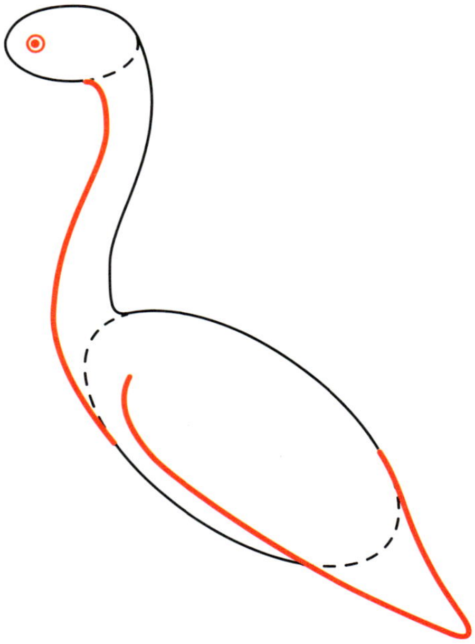

4.

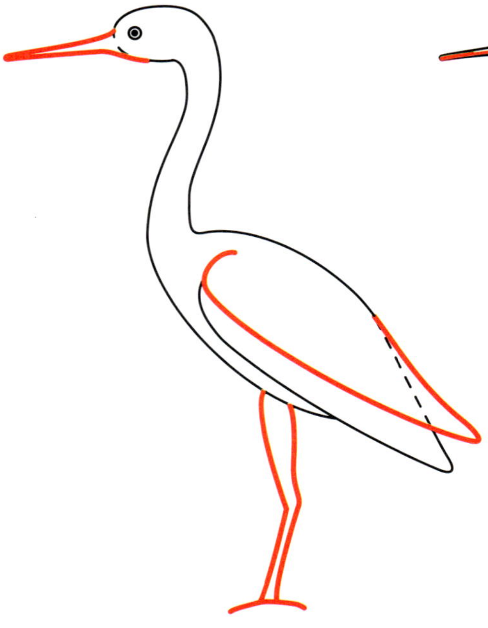

5.

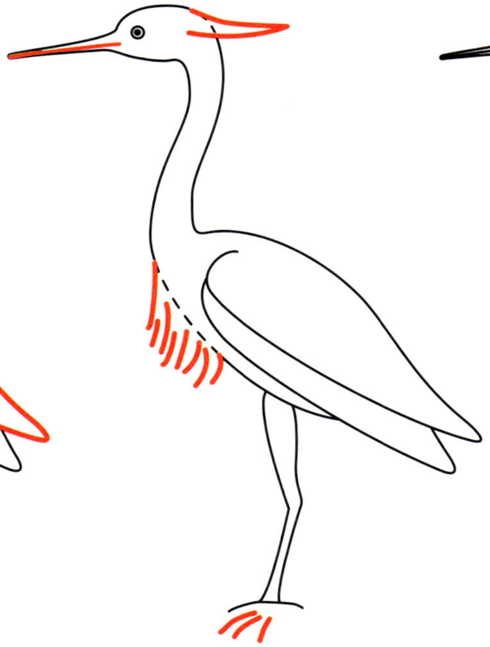

6.

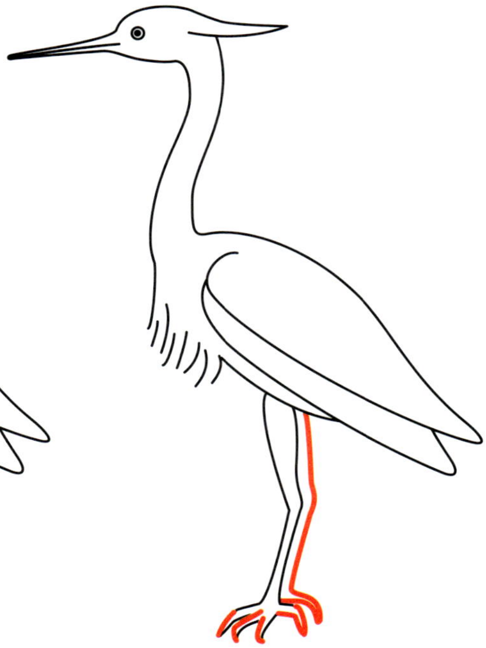

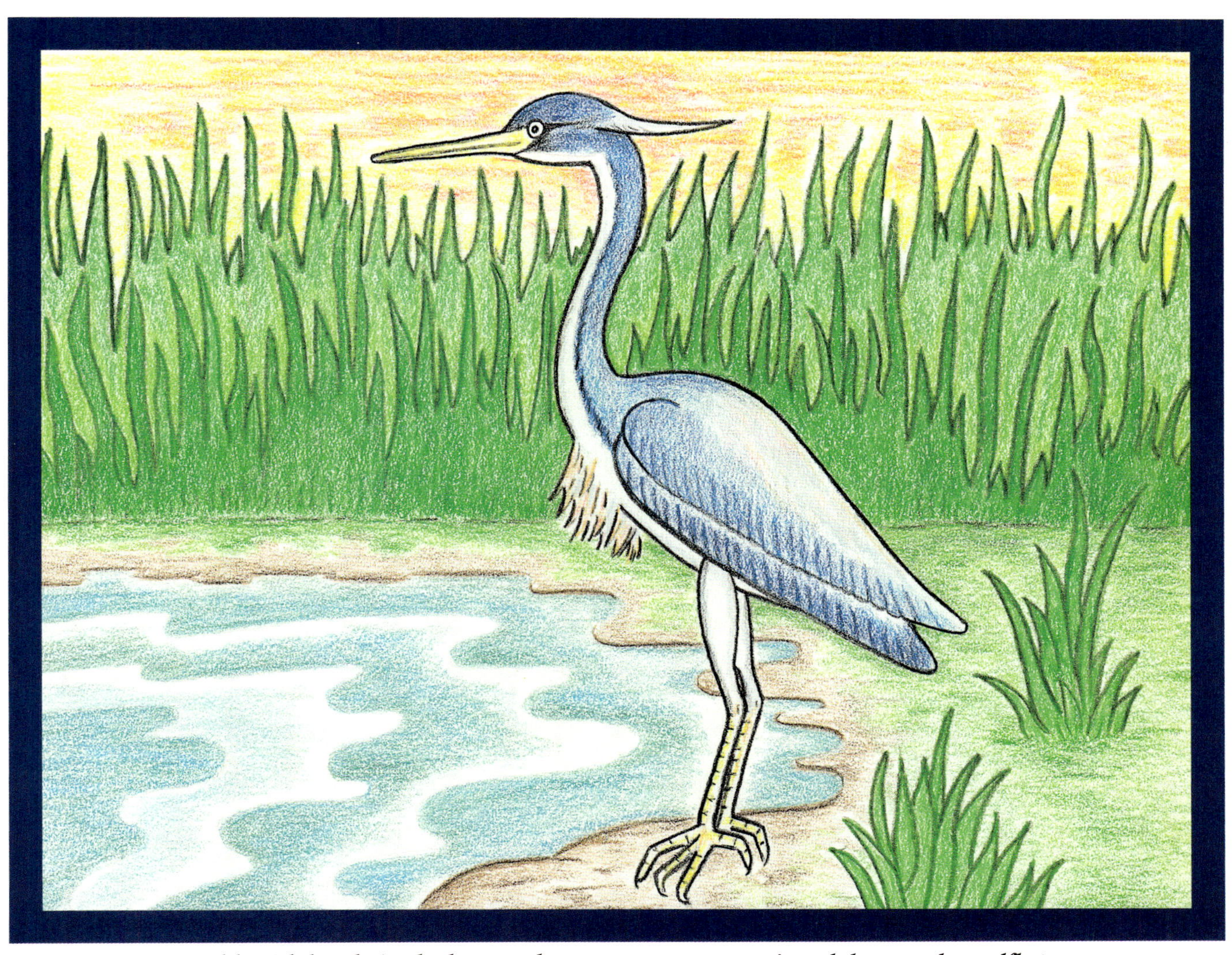

Muddy tidelands include marshes, swamps, estuaries, deltas and mudflats.

Ocean water rises on tidelands.
It covers the land twice a day.
Some tidelands are muddy.
They are saltwater wetlands.

Do animals live in mud?

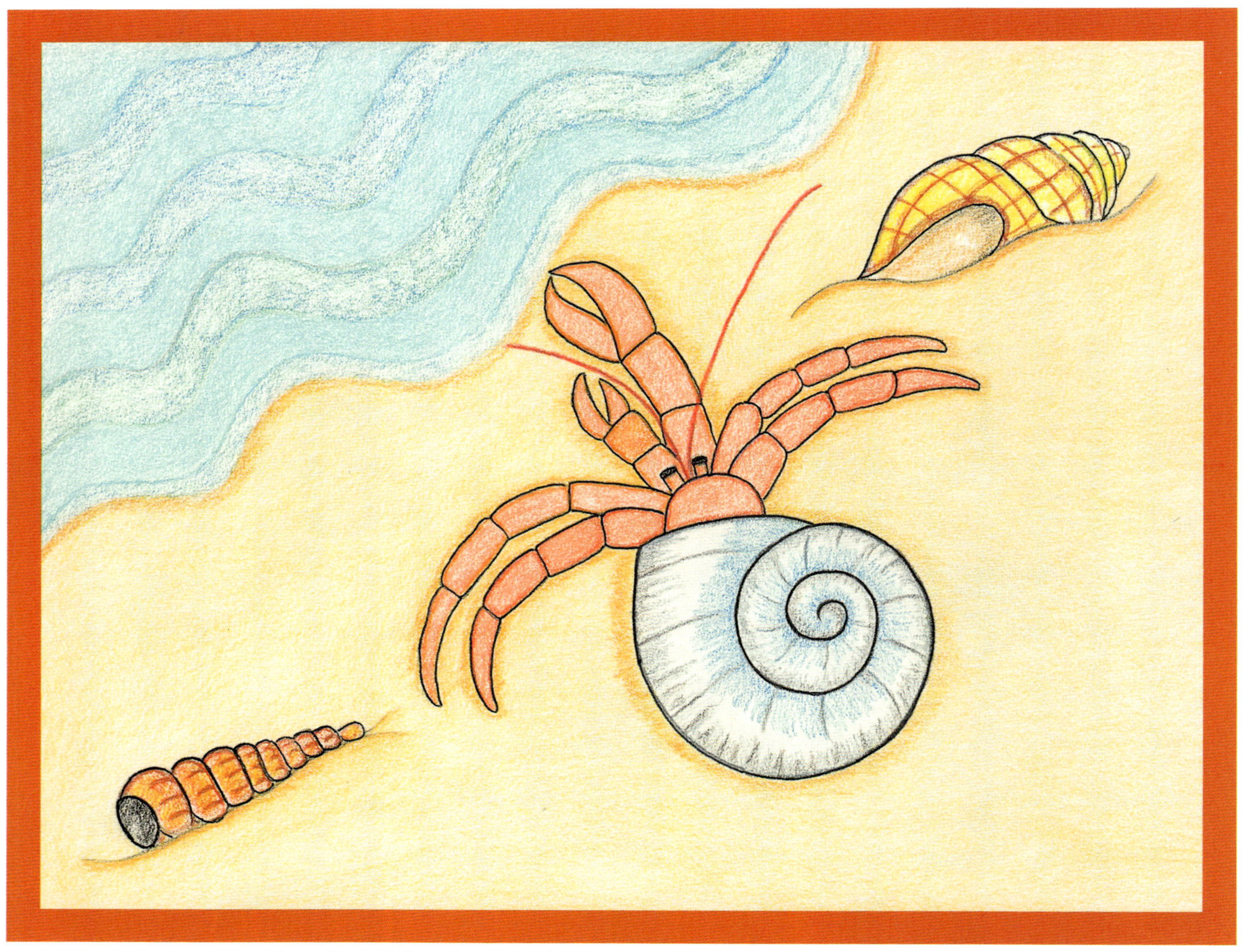

Sandy tidelands include sandy shores and sandy beaches.

Some tidelands are sandy.
Waves smooth the sand.
Hermit crabs visit beaches.
They search for seashells.

Where do seashells come from?

Question answered on page 62

Hermit Crab

1.

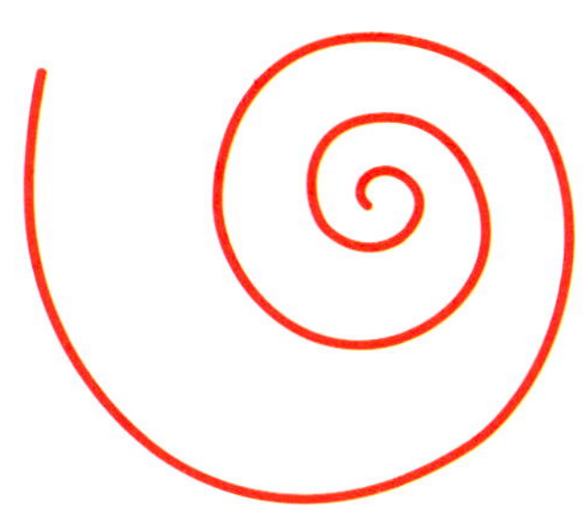

2.

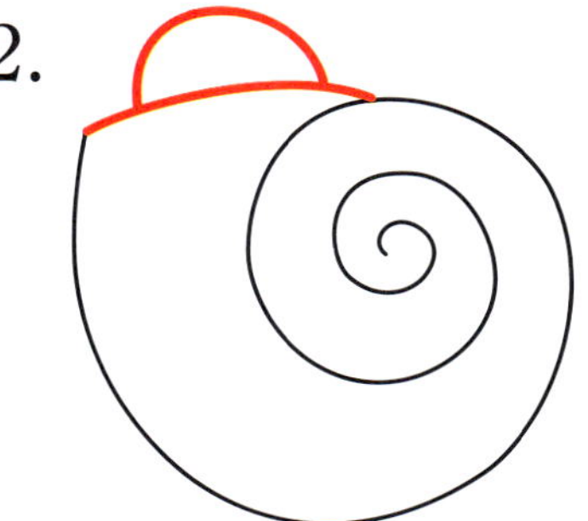

3.

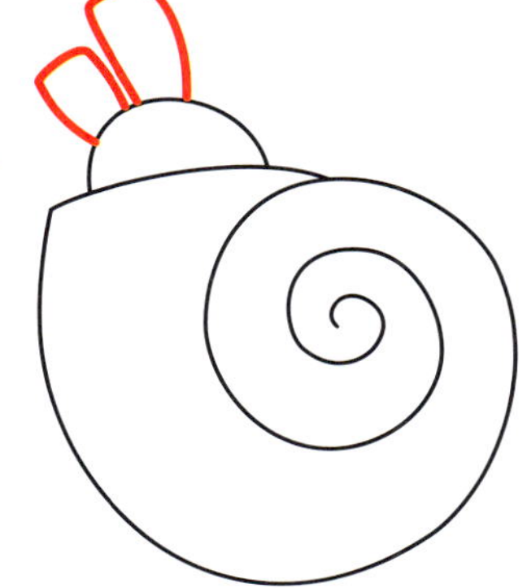

4.

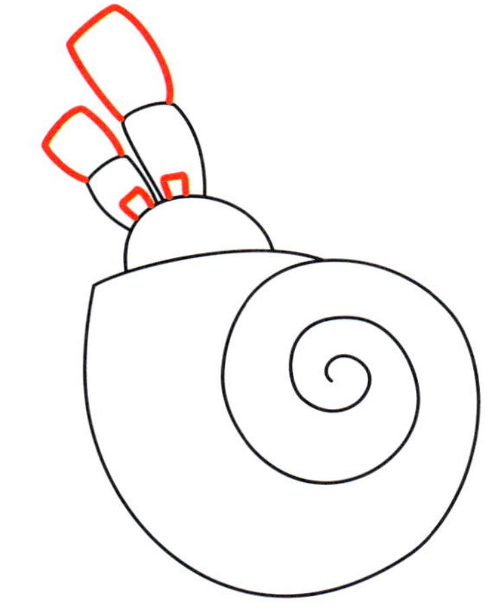

5.

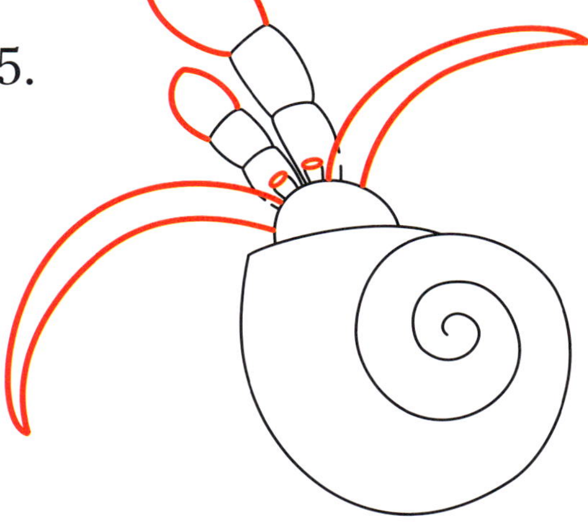

6.

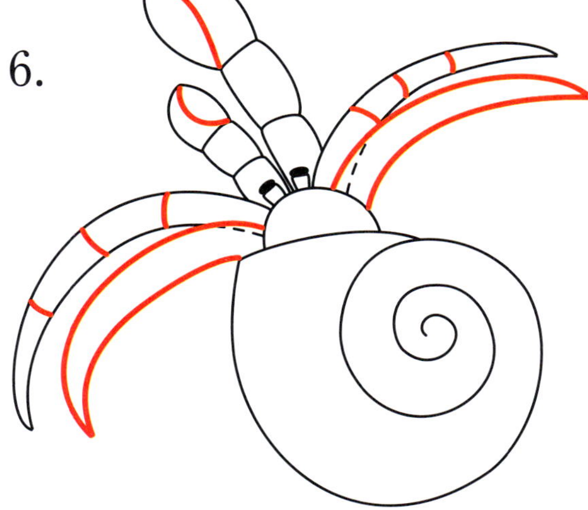

7.

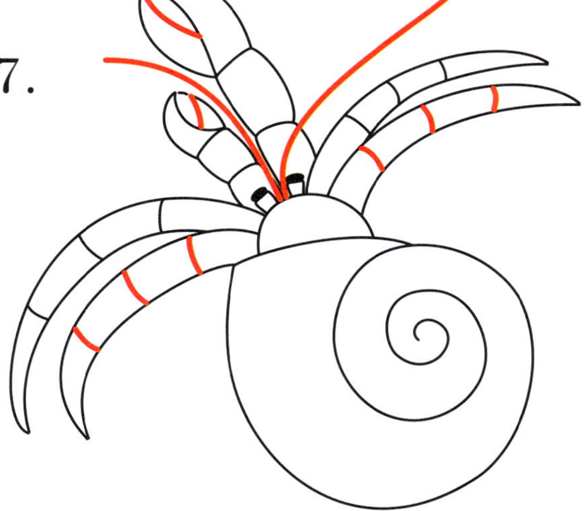

Rocky Tidelands

Question answered on page 62

Starfish (Sea Star)

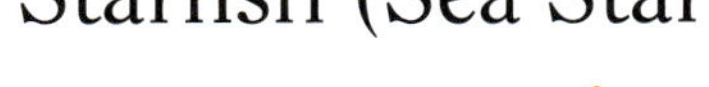

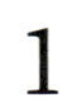

1.

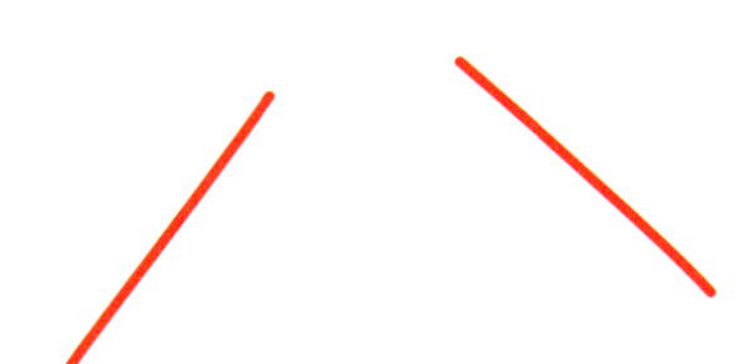

2.

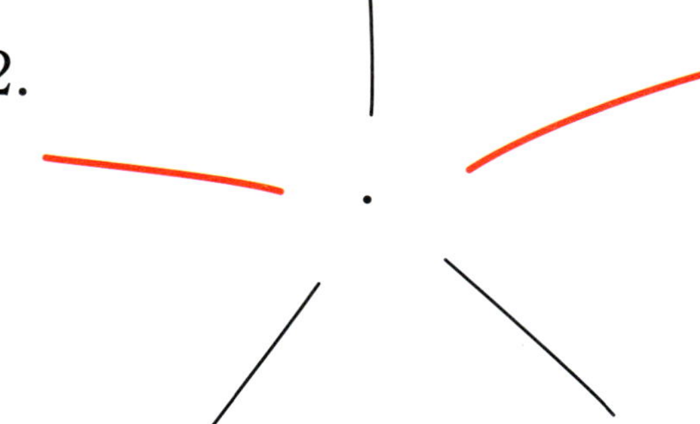

3.

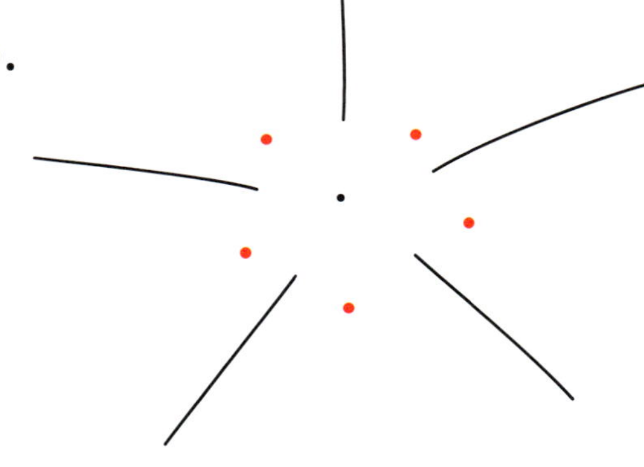

4.

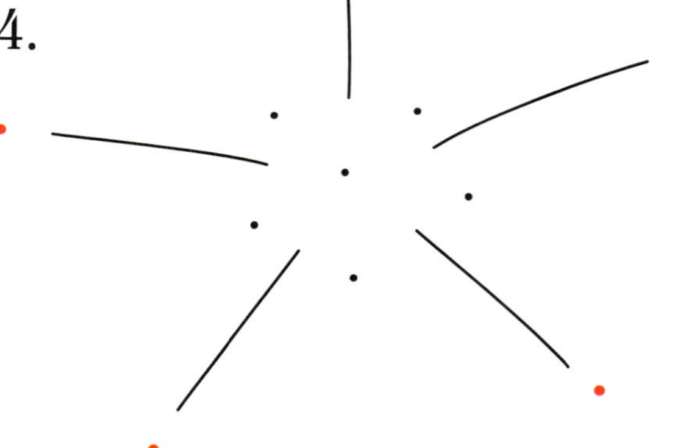

5.

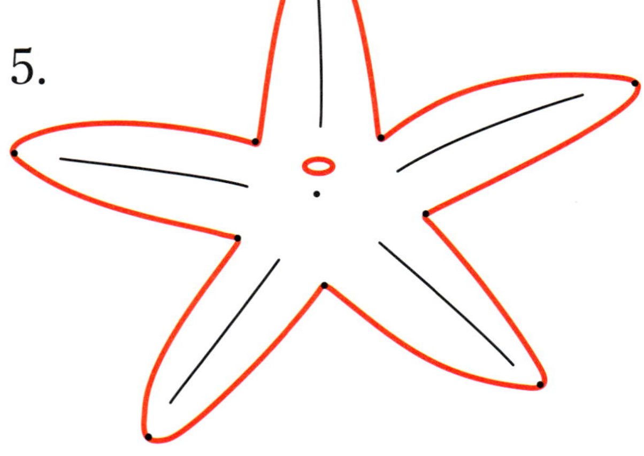

6.

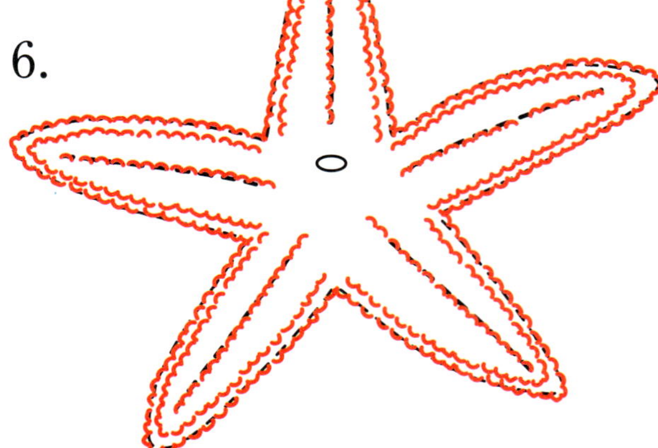

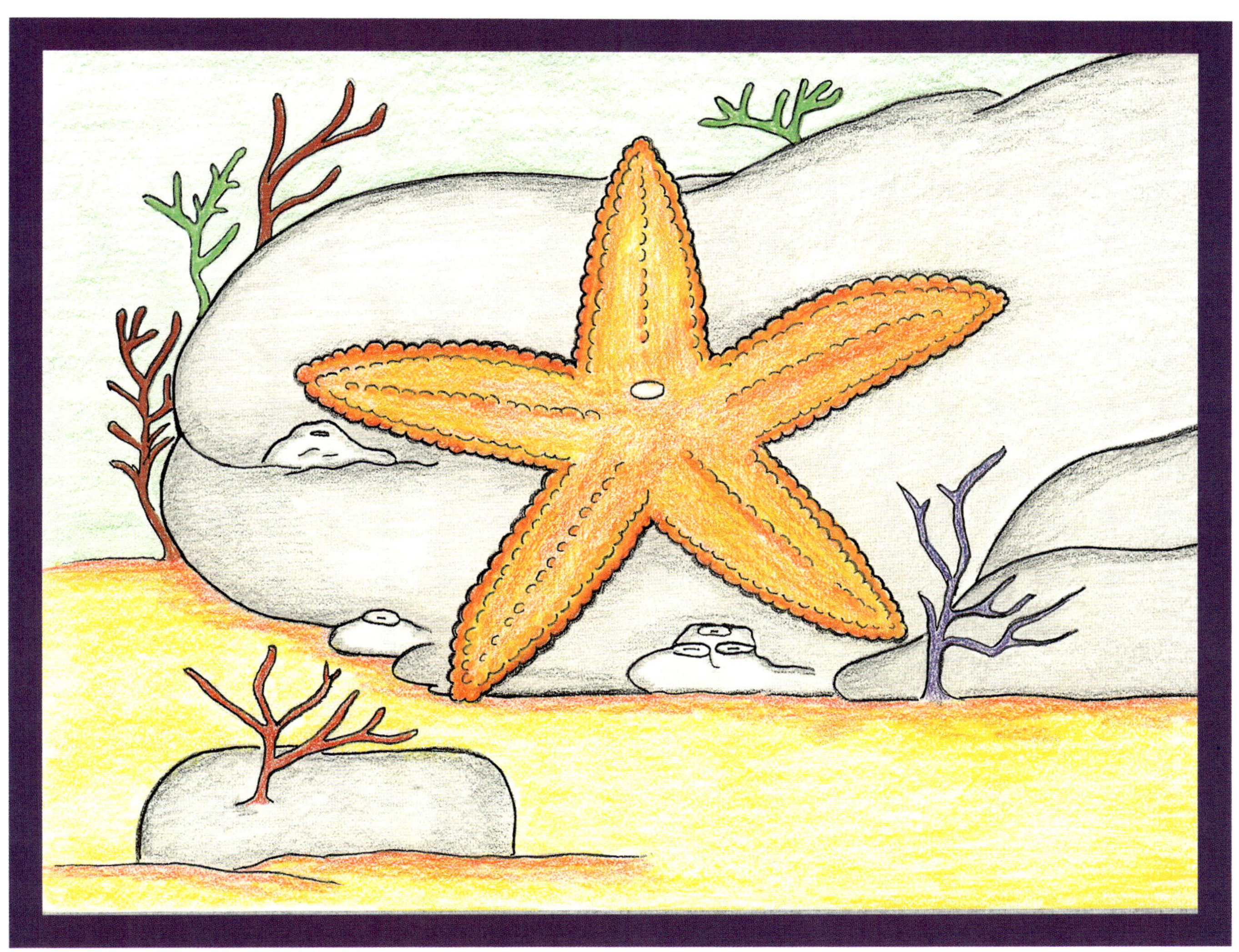

Rocky tidelands include rocky shores, rocky beaches and rocky coastlines.

Some tidelands are rocky.

Waves crash against the rocks.

Many rocky beaches have pools.

Starfish cling to the rocks.

What other animals cling to their rocky homes?

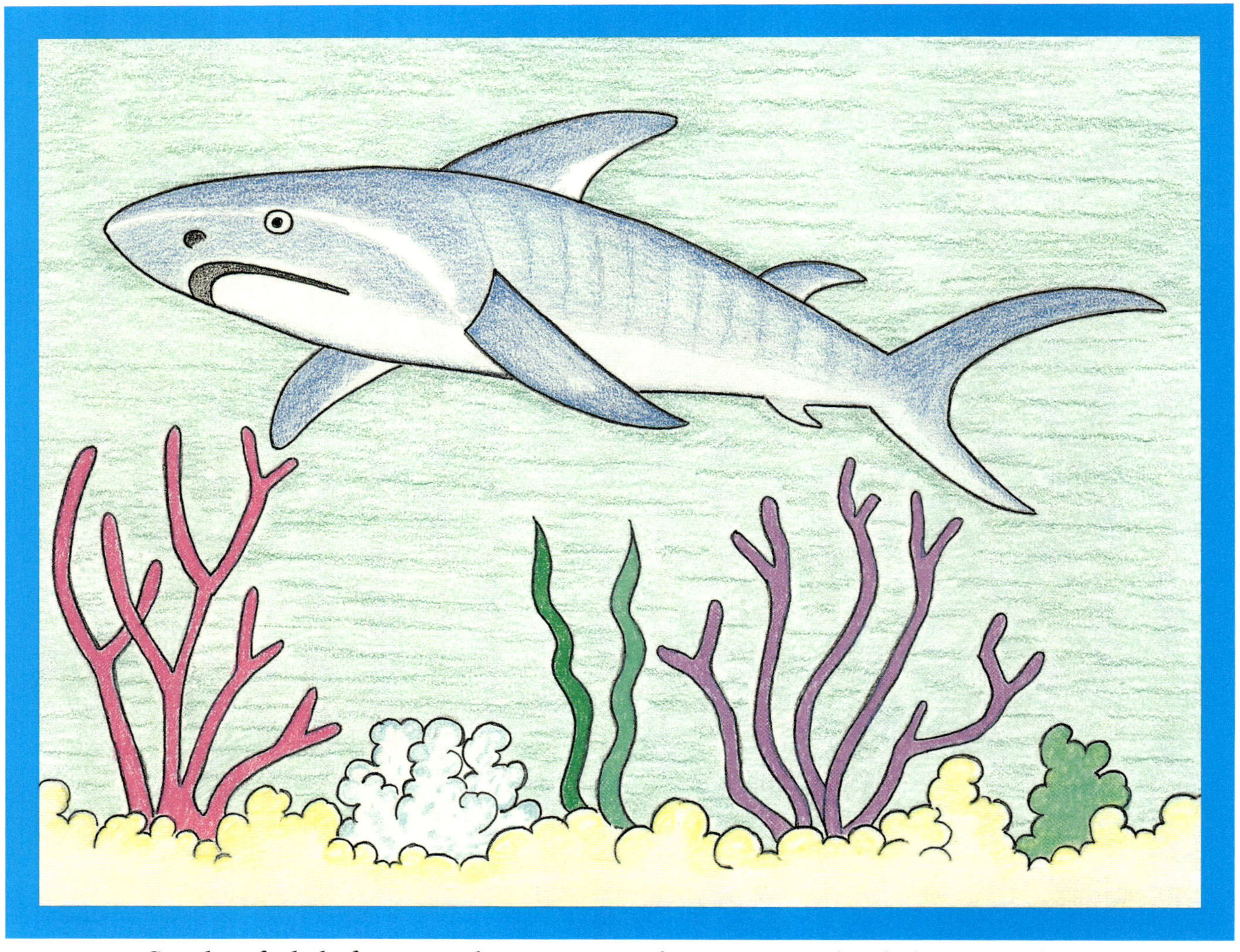

Coral reefs, kelp forests and seagrass meadows grow on the shelves near shore.

Land slopes down into the ocean.
It is covered by water.
These areas are called shelves.
Many animals live here.

Land
Coral, kelp or seagrass
Shelf
Open ocean
Deep open ocean

Why are the shelves home to many sea animals?

Shelves

Question answered on page 62

Shark

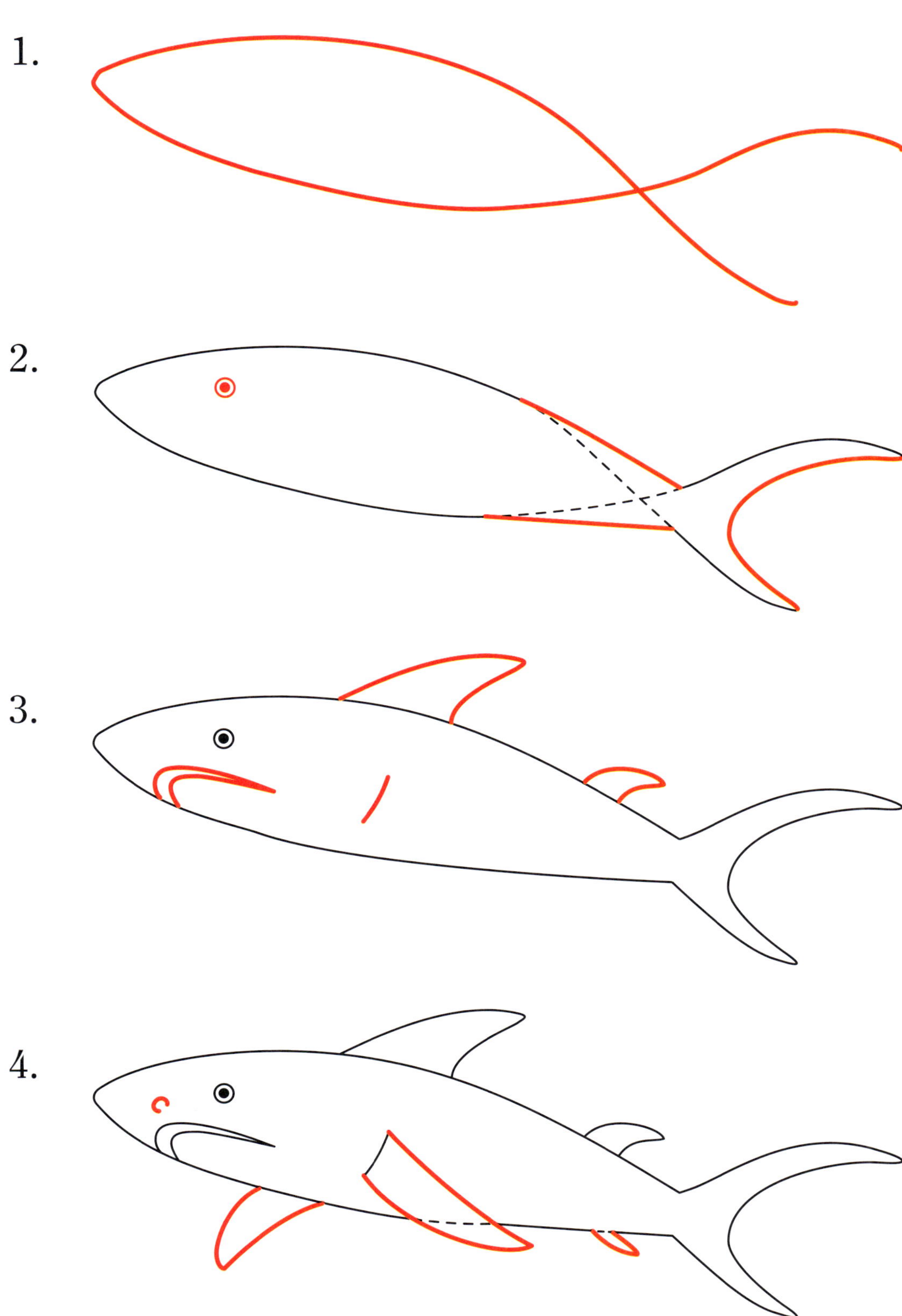

Outer Shelves

Question answered on page 62

Octopus

1.

2.

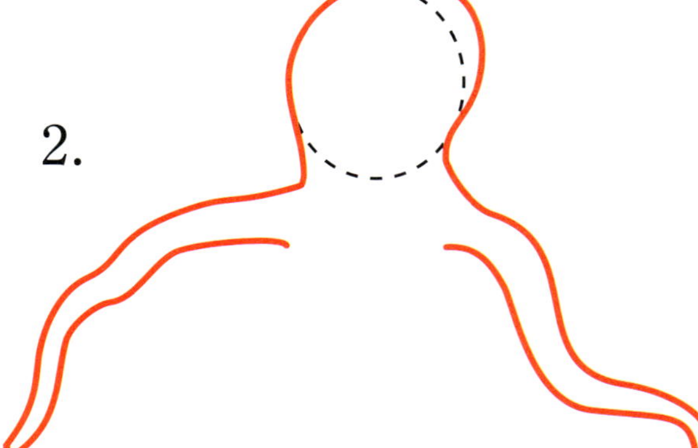

3.

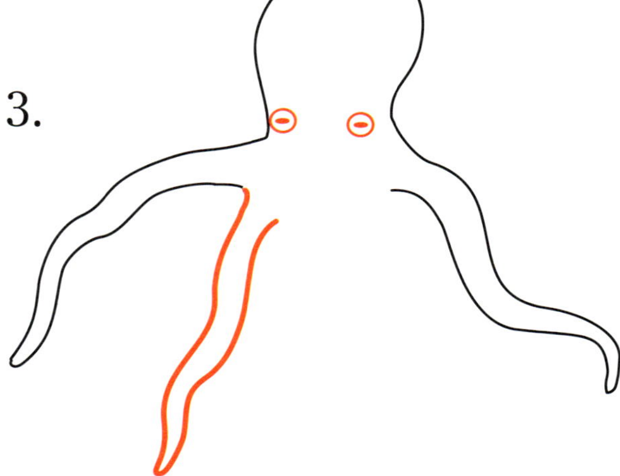

4.

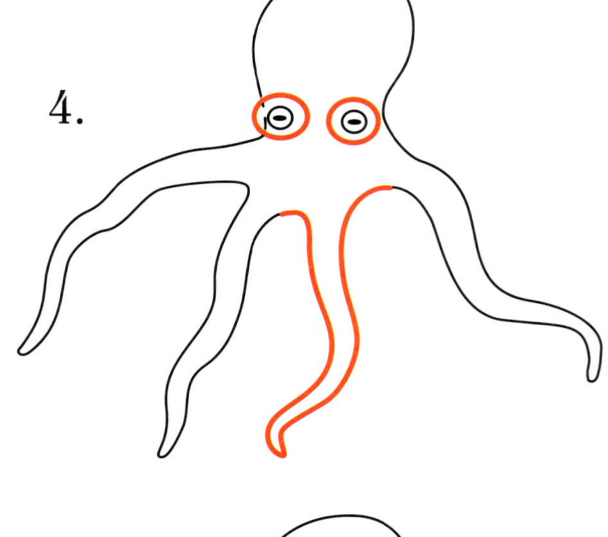

5.

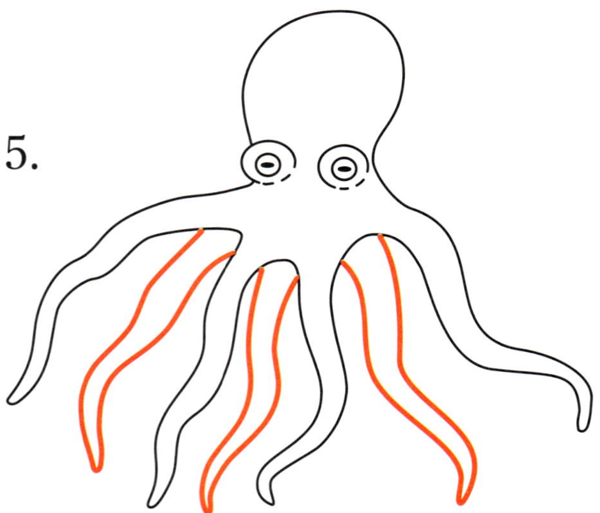

6.

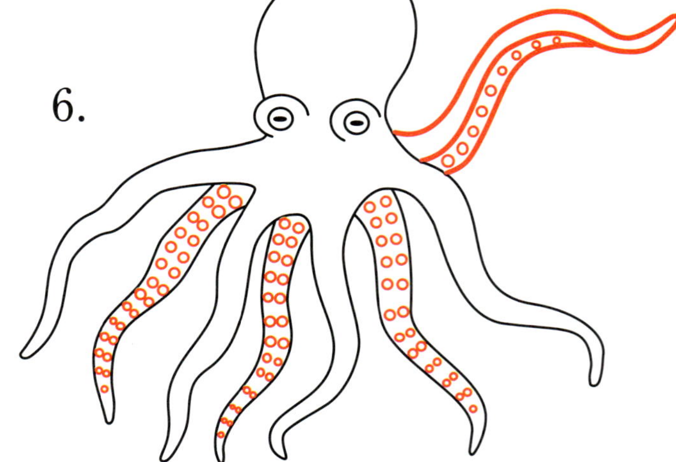

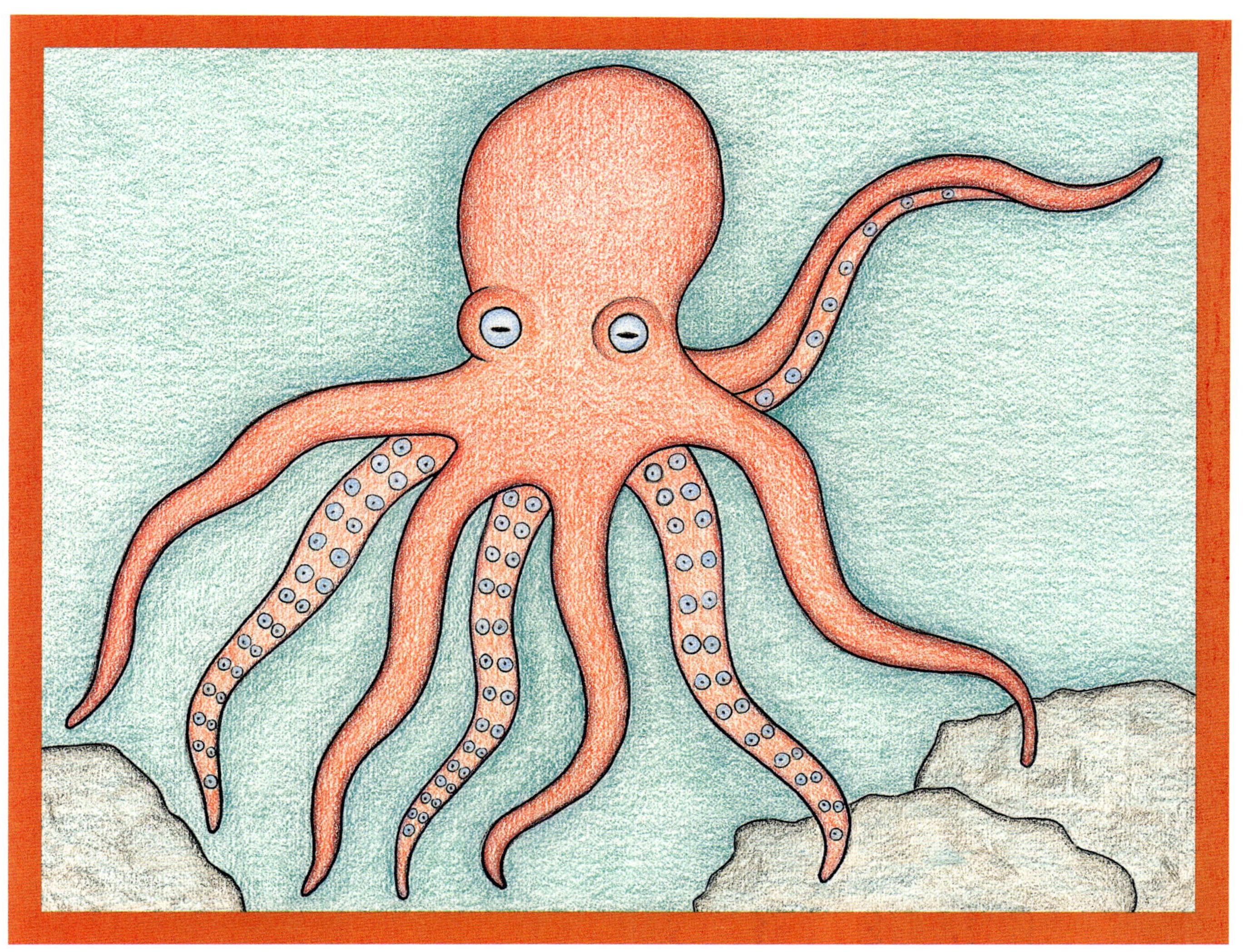

The ocean shelves are called the continental shelves.

The shelves slope downward.
The outer shelf water is deep.
Octopi live on the shelves.
They squeeze into tiny places.

What does an octopus eat?

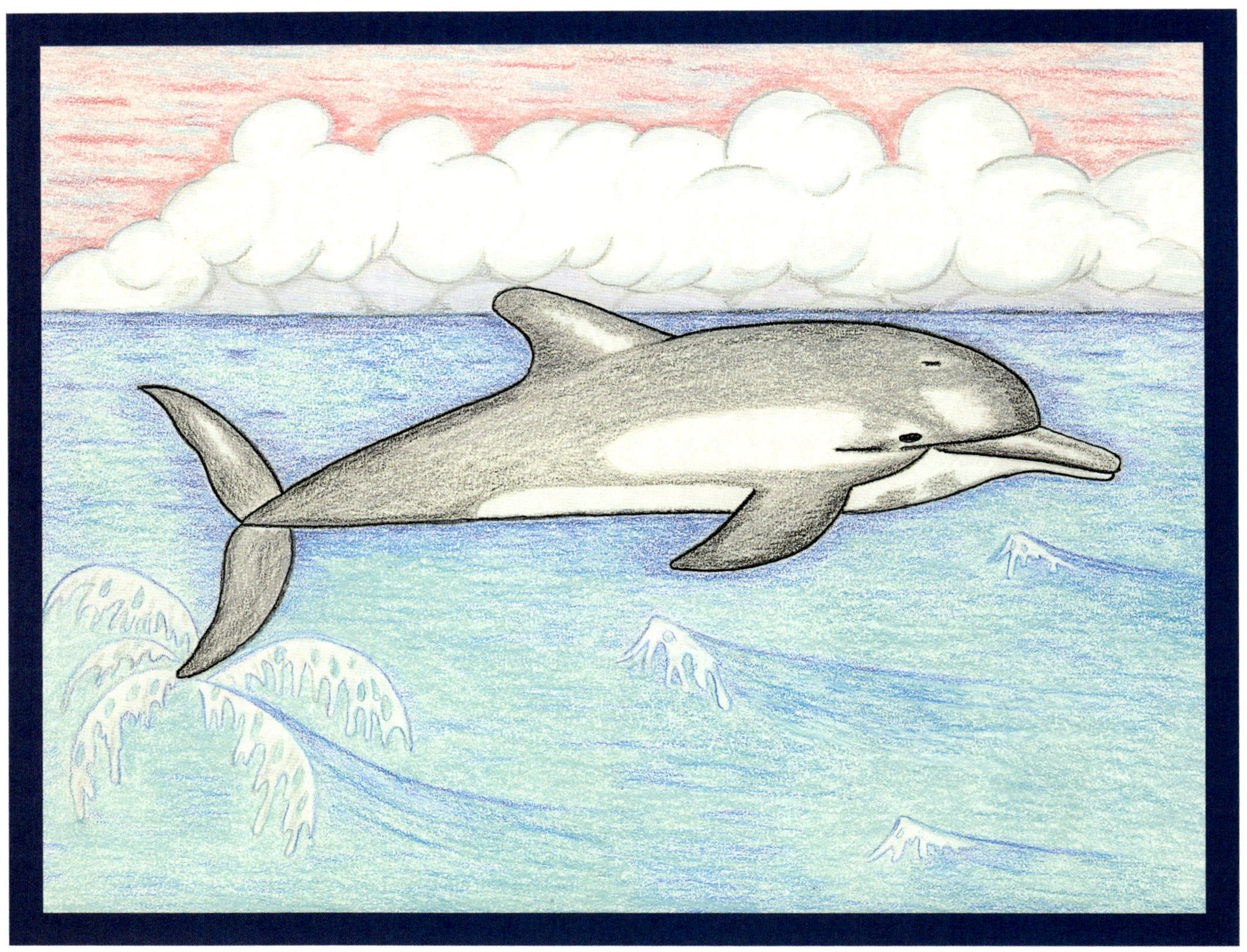

The sunlit open ocean is sometimes called "blue water".

The open ocean is far from land.
Sunshine enters the upper water.
Jellyfish drift in the water.
Dolphins zip through it.

Do whales live in the open ocean?

Sunlit Open Ocean

Question answered on page 62

Dolphin

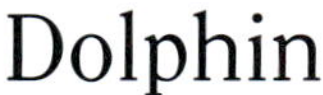

1.

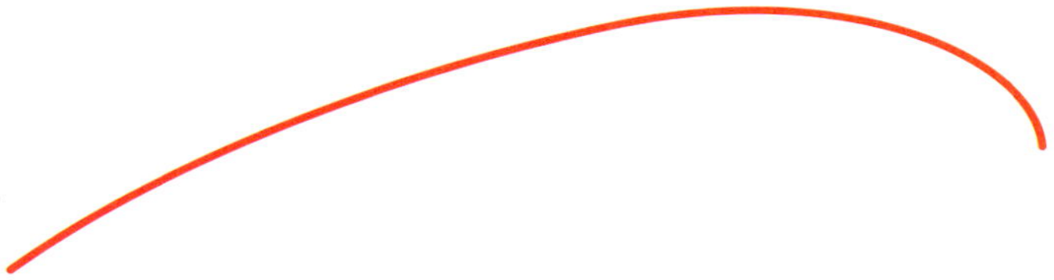

2.

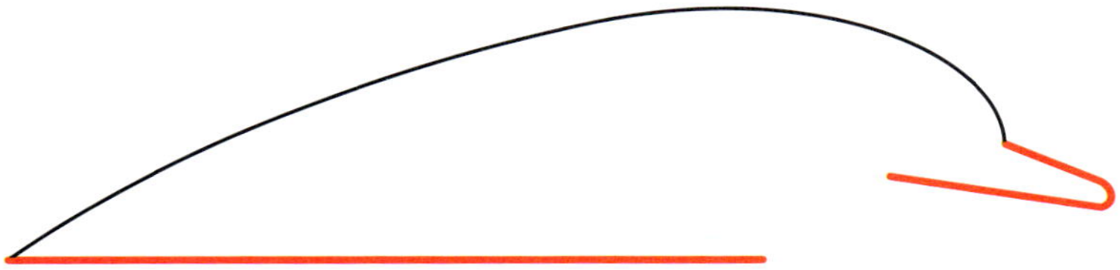

3.

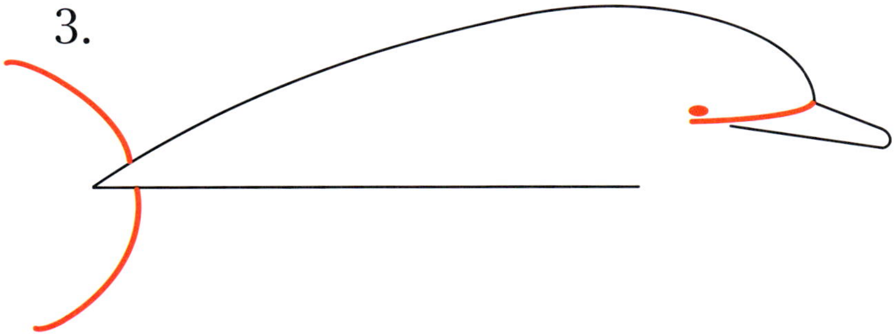

4.

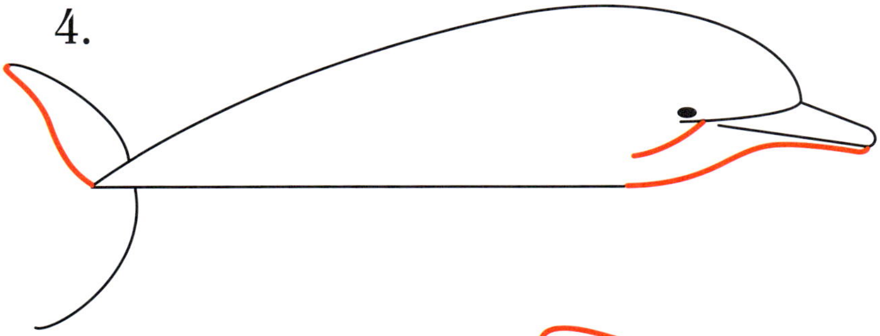

5.

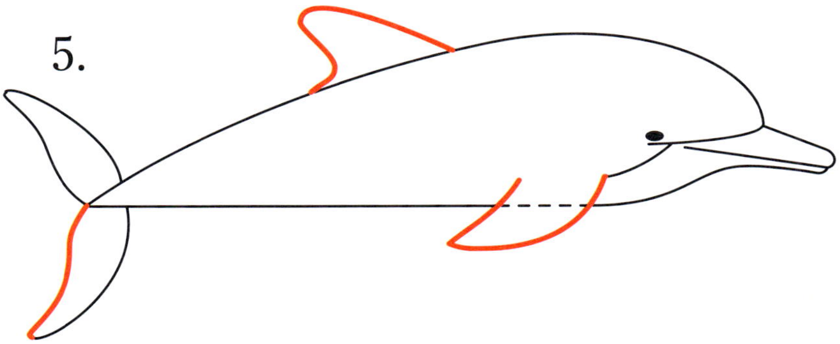

Deep Open Ocean

Question answered on page 62

Angler Fish

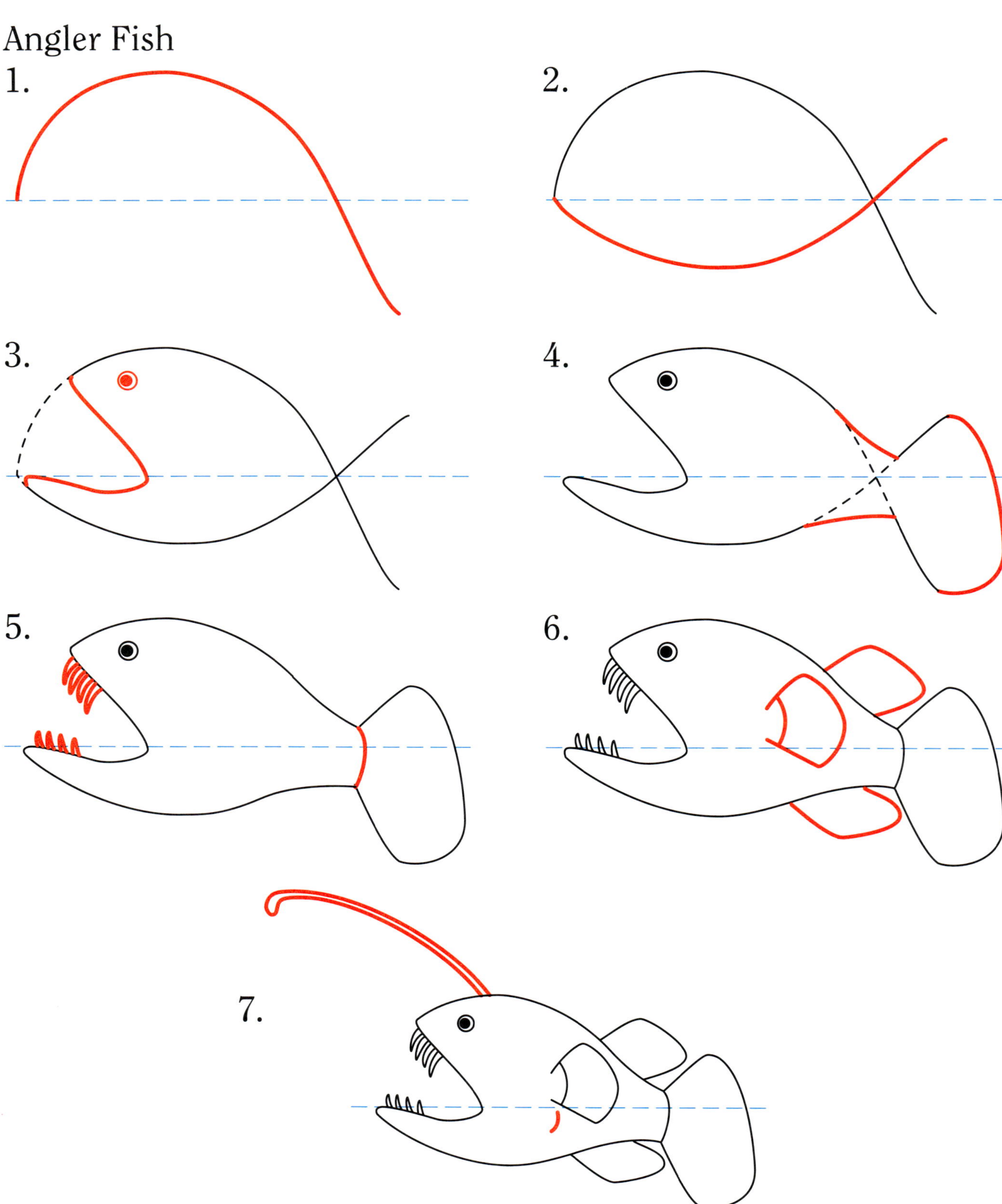

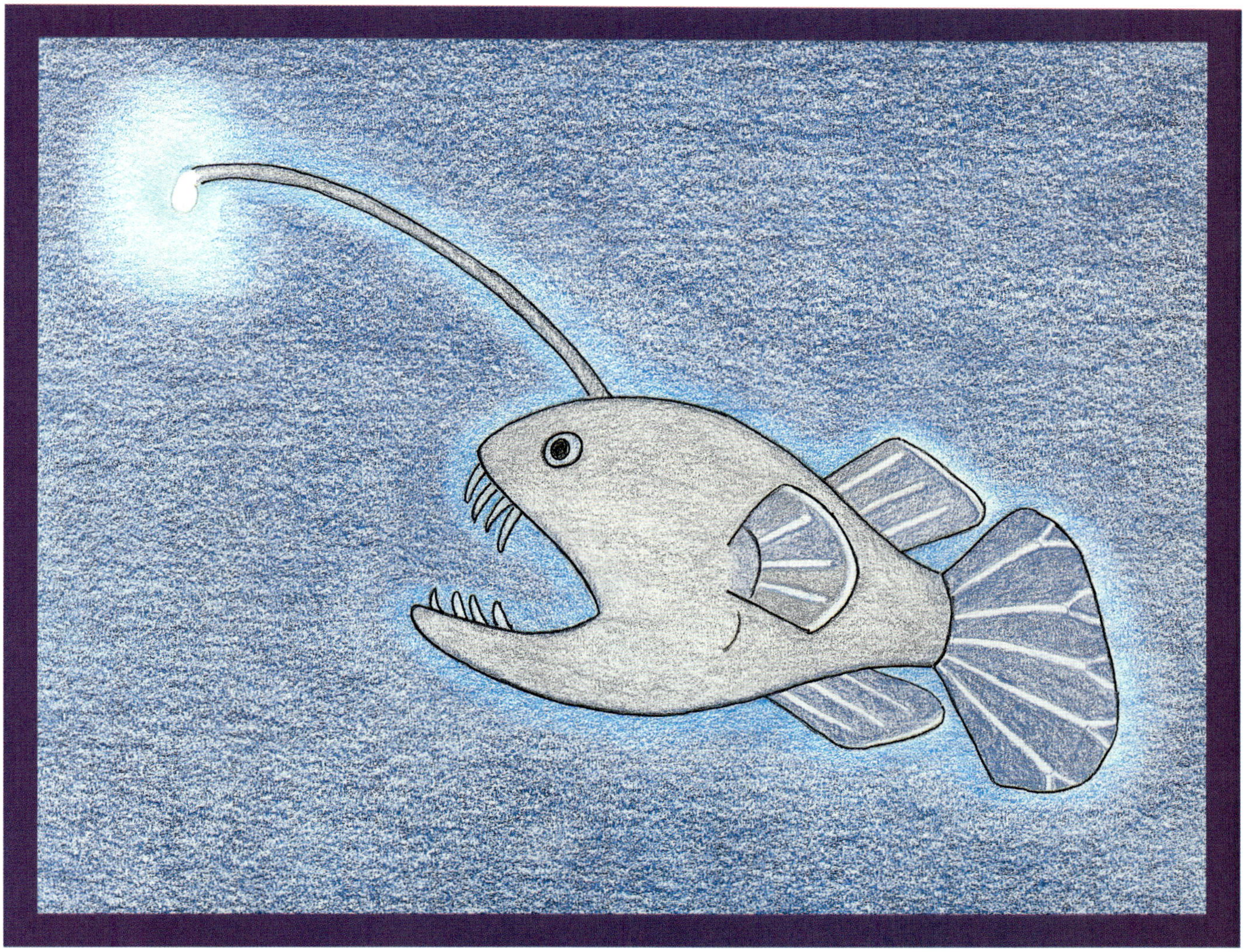

The deep open ocean is sometimes called "the deep sea" or "the deep".

The open ocean is very deep.
The bottom water is dark.
No sunlight reaches deep water.
Angler fish have their own light.

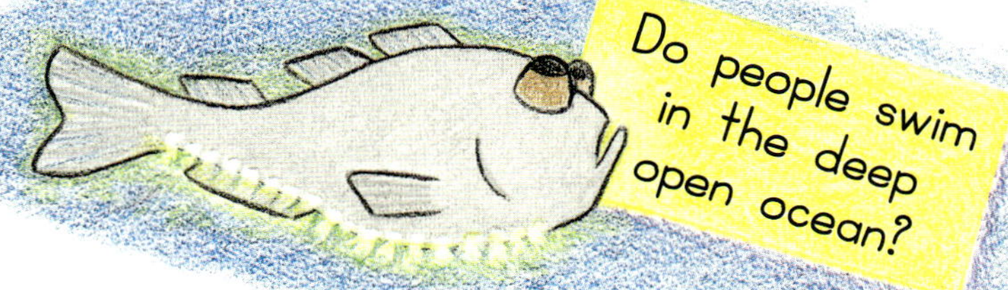

Draw From Your Imagination

Pretend you are a scuba diver . . .

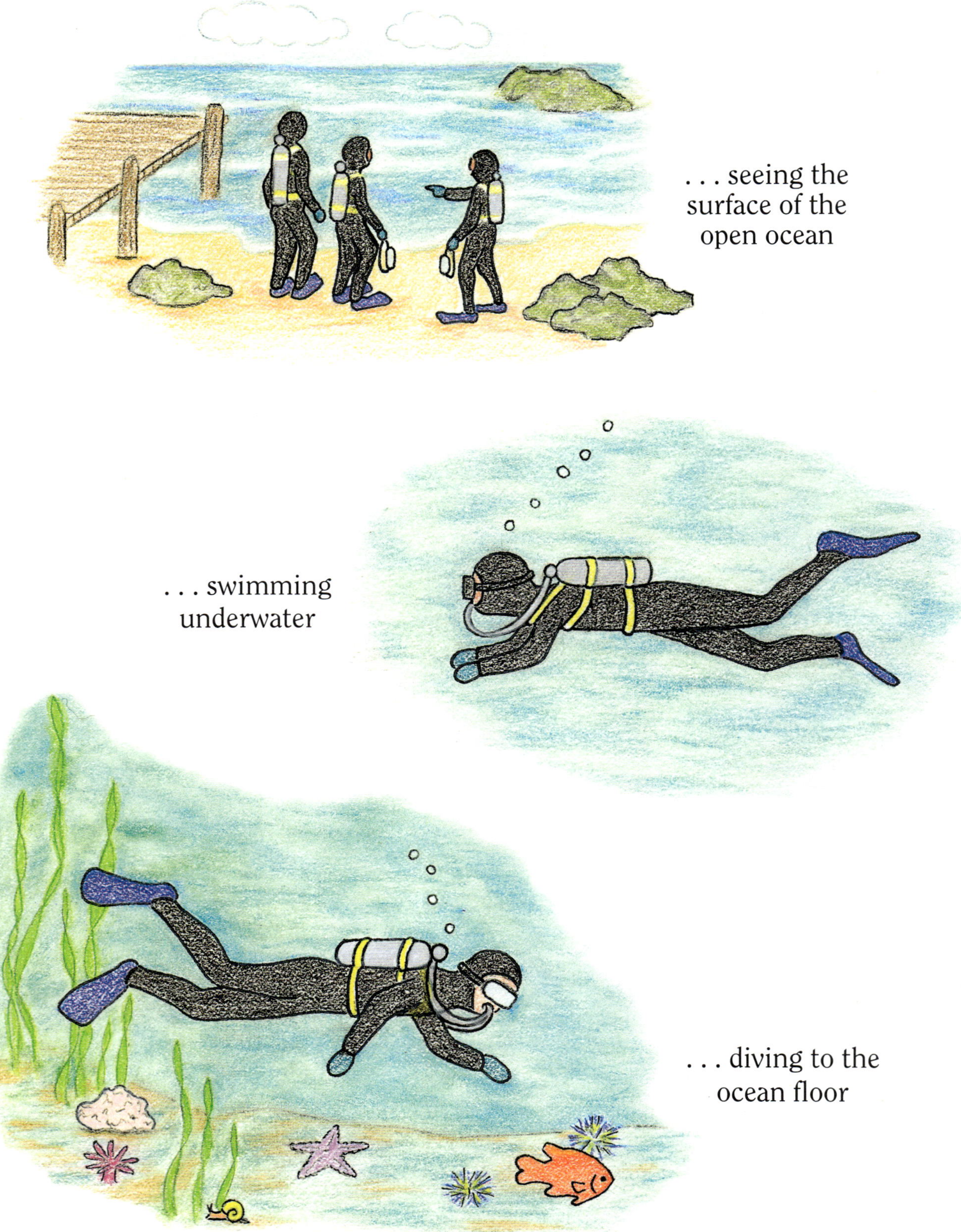

. . . seeing the surface of the open ocean

. . . swimming underwater

. . . diving to the ocean floor

Start your background with a line . . .

Draw a line to show the surface of the water.

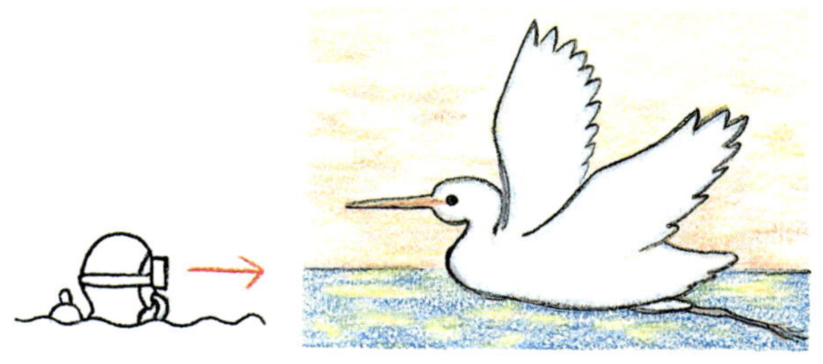

Mostly Sky

(page 36)

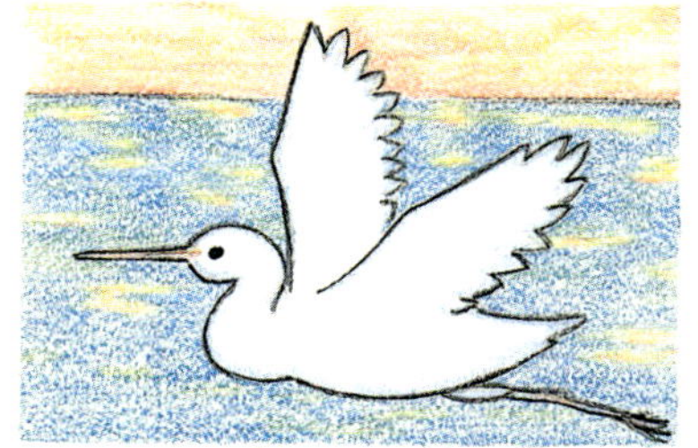

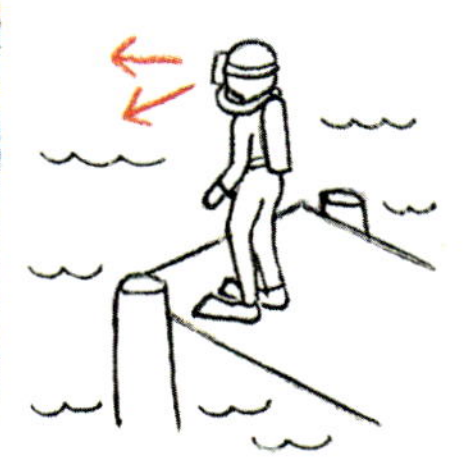

Mostly Water

(page 56)

Draw a line to show the ocean floor.

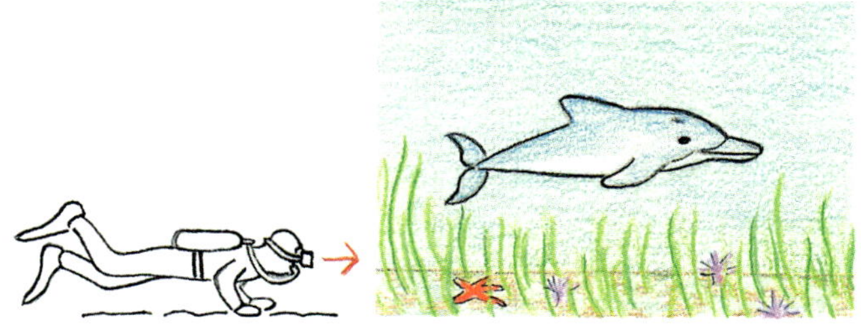

Mostly Water

(pages 39 and 52)

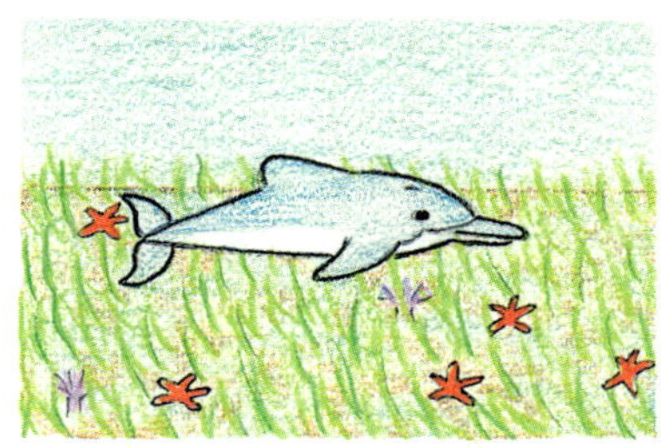

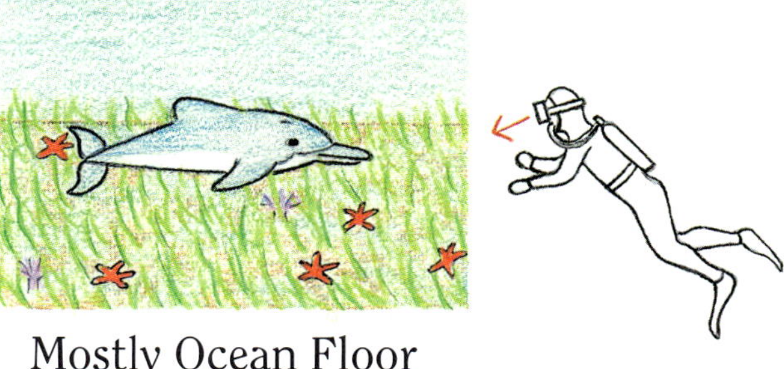

Mostly Ocean Floor

(pages 51 and 55)

Or, draw your background without a line.

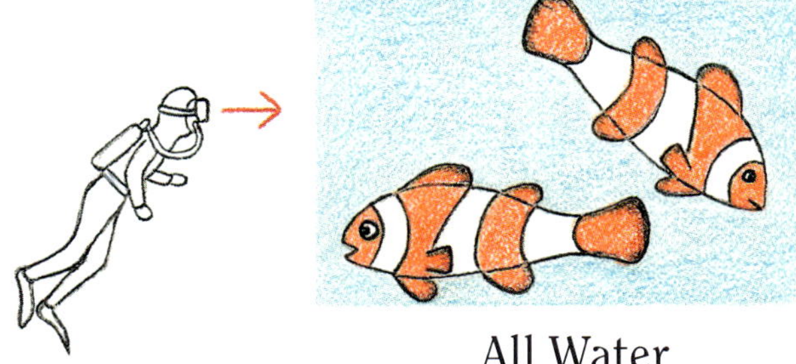

All Water

(pages 32 and 58)

Look at an aquarium . . .

An aquarium is like a minature pond, lake or ocean.
When you look in an aquarium, you can see...

- the sky above the water
- the surface of the water
- the water (is it freshwater or saltwater?)
- the surface of the ground
- underground.

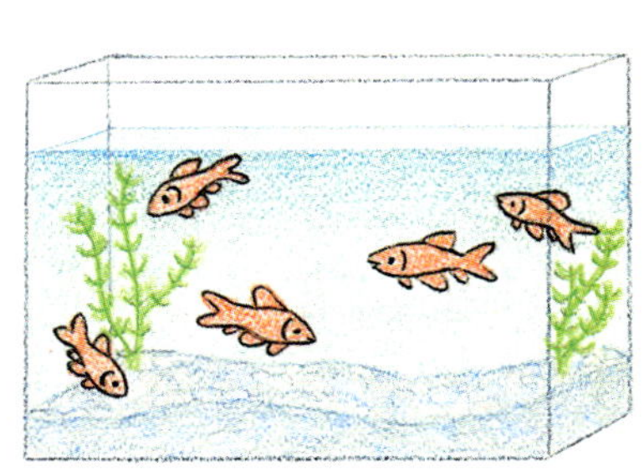

(page 35 and the cover of this book)

Learn more about oceans...

SHOULD PEOPLE DRINK OCEAN WATER? Page 44

No, it would make you sick, but sponges and other marine animals couldn't live without it. The water in the ocean is full of free-floating, one-celled plants called phytoplankton. See how ocean animals depend on this microscopic plant with THIS IS THE SEA THAT FEEDS US *by Robert Baldwin, illustrated by Don Dyen, published by Dawn, 1998.*

The world's oceans are really one huge interconnected pool of water. Follow a toy boat as it travels on stormy waves in one ocean then floats through calm, tropical coral reefs in the next in ACROSS THE BIG BLUE SEA *written and illustrated by Jakki Wood, published by National Geographic Society, 1998.*

DO ANIMALS LIVE IN MUD? Page 47

Yes, worms, insect larvae, clams and soft-shelled crabs thrive in muddy tidelands. An artist and her daughter share the marsh, mudflats, forest, pond and sand near their home in AN ISLAND SCRAPBOOK *written and illustrated by Virginia Wright-Frierson, published by Simon & Schuster, 1998.*

WHERE DO SEASHELLS COME FROM? Page 48

A shell on a beach was once the underwater home of a sea snail. Learn about these portable homes with WHAT LIVES IN A SHELL? *by Kathleen Weidner Zoehgeld, illustrated by Helen K. Davie, published by HarperCollins, 1994. Then, follow a hermit crab as he searches for a new home in* IS THIS A HOUSE FOR HERMIT CRAB? *by Megan McDonald, illustrated by S.D. Schindler, published by Orchard, 1990.*

Waves bring sand to beaches, but severe storms remove it. See how a community rebuilds the beach in SUMMER SANDS *by Sherry Garland, illustrated by Robert Lee, published by Harcourt Brace, 1995.*

WHAT OTHER ANIMALS CLING TO THEIR ROCKY HOMES? Page 51

Barnacles, mussels, sea slugs, crabs and anemones are a few of the animals on a rocky beach. Read about a boy who finds a salmon stranded in a puddle on his rocky beach in A SALMON FOR SIMON *by Betty Waterton, illustrated by Ann Blades, published by Douglas & McIntyre, 1980.*

WHY ARE THE SHELVES HOME TO MANY SEA ANMIMALS? Page 52

Sea animals gather along the shelves because there is lots of food! The shelves are like undersea nurseries for fish and plants. See OUR WET WORLD *by Sneed B. Collard III, illustrated by James M. Needham, published by Charlesbridge, 1998.*

WHAT DOES AN OCTOPUS EAT? Page 55

Octopi eat crabs, sea snails and clams. Learn about these clever, quiet animals with GENTLE GIANT OCTOPUS *by Karen Wallace, illustrated by Mike Bostock, published by Candlewick Press, 1998.*

Learn more about what lives on the bottom of the ocean with THE MAGIC SCHOOL BUS ON THE OCEAN FLOOR *by Joanna Cole, illustrated by Bruce Degen, published by Scholastic, 1992.*

DO WHALES LIVE IN THE OPEN OCEAN? Page 56

Whales use the open ocean to get from one continental shelf to another continental shelf. Learn how the open oceans provide passage for migrating tuna, sea turtles and other marine animals with THEY SWIM THE SEAS *by Seymour Simon, illustrated by Elsa Warnick, published by Harcourt Brace, 1998.*

DO PEOPLE SWIM IN THE DEEP OPEN OCEANS? Page 59

Special vehicles are required for humans to get to and be in the deepest ocean waters, so it is visited by only about 50 scientists worldwide. Get a glimpse at earth's last frontier with BENEATH BLUE WATERS *by Deborah Kovacs & Kate Madin, photographed by Larry Madin, published by Viking, 1996.*

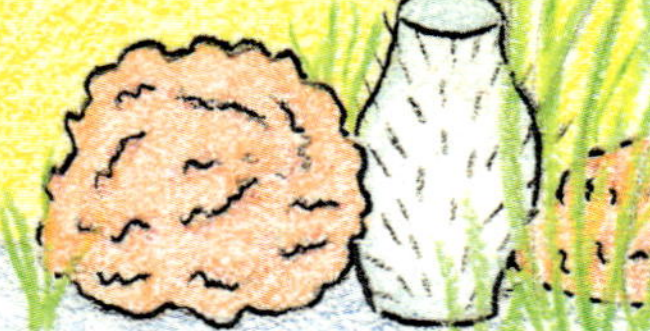

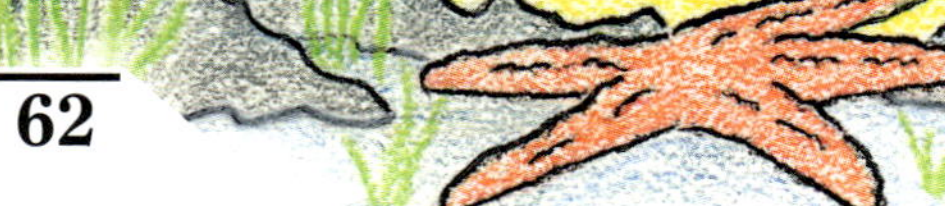

Teaching Tips

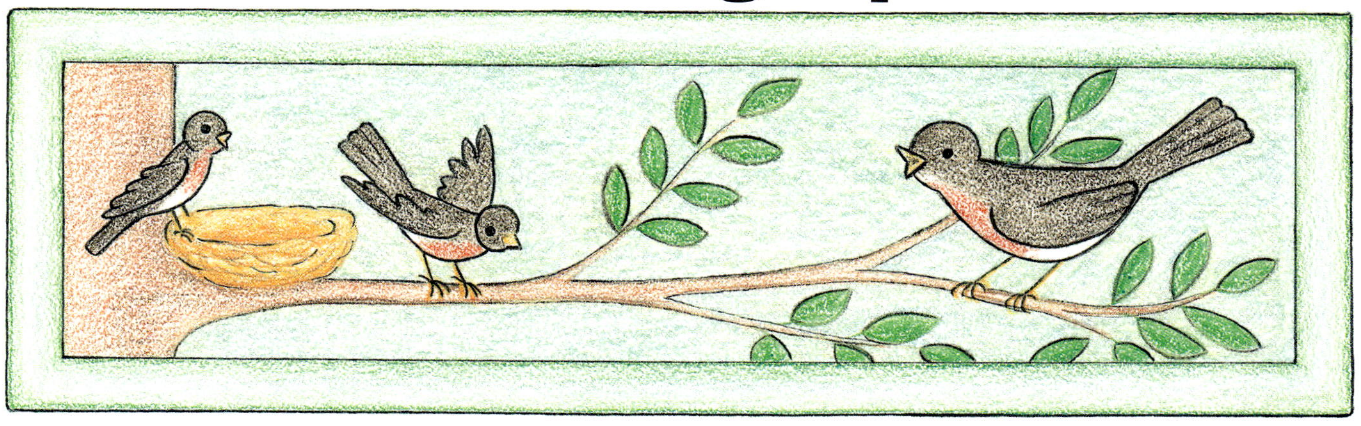

On Land

Some animals prefer to live among trees, others prefer to live on ice. Animals have many natural environments to choose from.

Here are Earth's major land biomes:

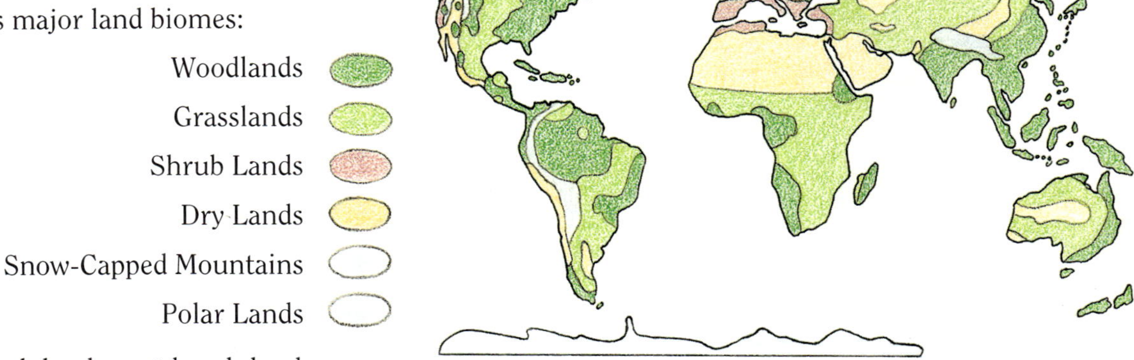

In this book, scrub lands, sagebrush lands and brush lands are included with deserts under "Dry Lands" (see page 18).

SHRUB LANDS • JACKRABBIT (page 16) —Describe the front of the hind leg (step 3) as a large number "2".

MOUNTAINS • MOUNTAIN GOAT (page 20) — Lightly predraw the parallelogram (step 1) on the children's papers. If you use $8\frac{1}{2}$" x 11" or 9" x 12" drawing paper, the recommended size of the parallelogram is 4" x $2\frac{1}{4}$".

Ponds & Rivers

All plants and animals need water. Clouds bring the water to land from the oceans. Streams and rivers carry the water back to the oceans. Some water pools on land in lakes or ponds.

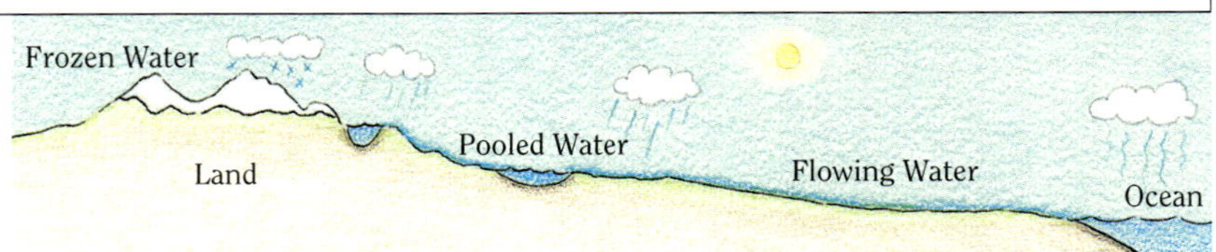

SHALLOW WATER • FROG (page 30)— Lightly predraw the triangle (step 1) on the children's papers. If you use $8\frac{1}{2}$" x 11" or 9" x 12" drawing paper, the recommended size of the isosceles triangle is 6" x 6" x $8\frac{1}{2}$".

DEEP WATER • FISH (page 33)—This lesson is simple and can easily be adapted to create a variety of fresh-water and marine fish. For examples, refer to the shark (page 53) and the angler fish (page 58).

OCEAN TO RIVER TO STREAM • EEL (page 38)—This lesson encourages full arm movement. The looped line (step 1) must be one smooth, continuous line. Ask the children to practice "drawing" the line in the air several times. Next, have the children move their finger to the paper surface and practice "drawing" the line again. Finally, have the children pick up their pencils and draw the line on their papers. When drawing the opposite side of the eel (step 2), tell the children to use the first line (step 1) as a guideline and to keep looking at their guideline — not their pencil point — as they draw. When drawing the fins (steps 3 and 4), remind the children to keep their eyes on the first and second line (step 1 and 2) for guidance.

Oceans

The oceans have many environments. Marine animals live in waters which may be cold, warm, shallow or deep. Rivers and streams deposit nutrients, soil and sand into the oceans.

Tideland
Island
Land
Shelf
Open ocean
Deep open ocean

MUDDY TIDELANDS • GREAT BLUE HERON (page 46) — Describe the neck (step 1) as a large number "2" that is tipped a little. This lesson is similar to the swan lesson in ***Draw•Write•Now®, Book One***.